NORTHWEST TRAILS

by Ira Spring and Harvey Manning

A Hiker's and Climber's Overview-Guide
to National Parks and Wilderness Areas in
Wyoming • Montana • Idaho • Northern California
Oregon • Washington • British Columbia • Canadian Rockies

Maps: Helen Sherman

THE MOUNTAINEERS/Seattle

THE MOUNTAINEERS: Organized in 1906
". . . to explore and study the mountains,
forests, and watercourses of the Northwest."

©1974, 1982 by Ira Spring and Harvey Manning

Published by The Mountaineers
306 2nd Ave. W., Seattle, Washington 98119
First printing June 1982; second printing August 1984; third printing January 1988

Published simultaneously in Canada by
Douglas & McIntyre, Ltd.
1615 Venables Street
Vancouver, British Columbia V5L 2H1

Cover photo: Magog Lake and 11,870-foot Mt. Assiniboine,
   Canadian Rockies
Title page: Mt. Daniel and Lower Robin Lake, Alpine
   Lakes Wilderness, Washington

Printed in the United States of America

Library of Congress Cataloging in Publication Data
Spring, Ira.
      Northwest trails.

      Rev. ed. of: Wilderness trails Northwest. 1974
      Includes index.
      1. Hiking—Northwest, Pacific—Guide-books.
2. Mountaineering—Northwest, Pacific—Guide-books.
3. Northwest, Pacific—Description and travel—
1951-   —Guide-books.   I. Manning, Harvey.   II. Title.
GV199.42.N69S67   1982   796.5'22   81-22573
ISBN 0-89886-037-7   AACR2

CONTENTS

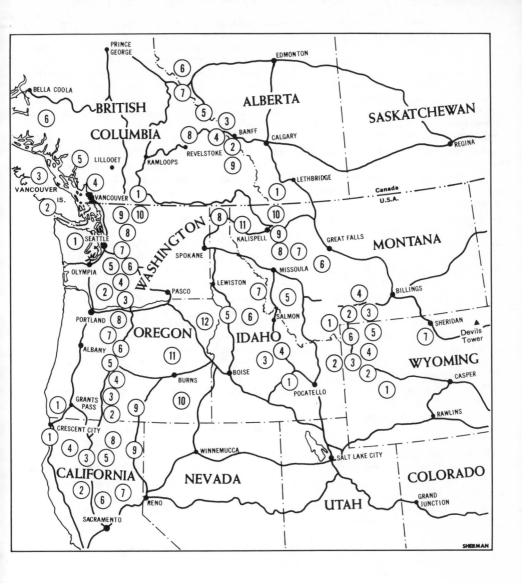

INTRODUCTION

A devout pedestrian whose home hills are the Cascades is bitten by the urge to roam afield. She is intrigued by Montana. But impressions from photographs and magazine articles and friends' stories blur in her mind. Where should she start? Glacier National Park? Beartooths? Madison Range? The Crazies?

A New Jersey walker-scrambler decides to blow his life savings on a summer vacation in the Northwest, sampling as many wildlands as possible. Since he may not be able to return for years he can't afford to waste a single day on less than the best. When he gets to the Olympics, which one hike will guarantee a rich taste of the special flavor? What peak should be his prime goal in the Wind River Range? How and where can he be initiated quickly into the quintessential Canadian Rockies?

For such situations and persons this book has been published—to provide an overview of hiking and climbing in the Pacific Northwest, defined for the present purpose as north-of-Sierra California, Oregon, Washington, Idaho, Wyoming, Montana, southern British Columbia, and the west edge of Alberta. Contiguity and other factors make this "Northwest" an entity distinguishable from the Colorado-California-Southwest region on one side, the northern British Columbia-Yukon-Alaska region on the other. Within it, however, lie as many differences as similarities.

For each of the wildland units presented here, photographs show the look of the country. Sketch maps give preliminary orientation. Text briefly describes the area and how to get there, tells if it is currently mobbed or lonesome, suggests representative hikes, notes whether the climbing is interesting and if so summarizes classic ascents, says what months the trails usually are sufficiently snowfree for hiking and the sort of weather to expect, and finally lists appropriate maps and (if any) guidebooks. Emphasis is on *overview*. For the fine detail needed to plan more than the briefest visit one must proceed beyond these pages to maps, guidebooks, hiking magazines, and climbing journals, to friends who have been there, and to the land managers (National Park Service, U.S. Forest Service, or other).

Though this book in effect is an inventory of Northwest wilderness currently protected and proposed for protection, the coverage is not complete. It is nearly so in northern California, Oregon, and Washington but gets a bit spotty in Idaho, Wyoming, and Montana, where conservationists have not yet finished their wilderness plan, and in the enormity of British Columbia merely hits representative points. For omitted areas, our apologies to the land and to the wildfolk striving to protect it from loggers, miners, dammers, subdividers, and the plague of ORV's (off-road vehicles) and ATV's (all-terrain vehicles), and, to use a less fancy term, "damn trailbikes."

The U.S. Forest Service has inventoried roadless areas in the National Forests of 5,000 acres or more and from these has chosen a number as New Wilderness Study Areas, to be submitted to a process of administrative review, public comment, and eventually legislative consideration for inclusion in the National Wilderness System. The Forest Service says that until final decisions are made these areas "will be protected from activities which would compromise their wilderness values." A few are described in the text, others are shown on the key maps to the individual states. The venturesome hiker is urged to obtain appropriate maps and plan his own investigations—and afterward submit testimony to the Forest Service and Congress, thus helping shape the future National Wilderness System.

It must be noted the Forest Service has omitted much de facto wilderness for which conservation organizations are seeking protection. Loss of an area to roads and logging must not be conceded simply because the Forest Service presently fails to include it on the study list. The public may seek to have an area added or, failing that, may proceed directly to Congress. That's what the Wilderness Society, Sierra Club, Friends of the Earth, and a host of regional and local groups are for—to give the public a loud voice.

A word is compulsory about outdoor manners. Every walker at every moment must take pains to minimize his and her impact on fragile ecosystems. Do not cut boughs for beds—carry a foam pad or air mattress. Do not build campfires in high country where the scarce wood (living *and* dead) is part of the scenery—carry a stove. If a fire is built, put it out afterward—forests should be burned by lightning, not man. Do not trench around tents and tarps—depend on ground sheet plus pad or mattress to keep sleeping bags dry. Do not camp in flower gardens or heather fields— go into the trees or onto moraine or river gravel. Do not pollute water—camp no closer than 100 feet to lakeshores and streambanks, wash bodies and dishes where soap or biodegradable detergent will enter the ground harmlessly. If privies are not available, eliminate body wastes far from watercourses and bury the evidence in a shallow hole—be as courteous as a cat. Do not toss garbage around and do not bury it either—

what cannot be burned in campfires, *carry out* of the wilderness, *all the way out*. (Remember that the hiker who throws fish guts and bacon grease in the bushes contributes to the delinquency of bears.) Do not shortcut trails and when in meadows follow established paths. In summary, be clean and quiet and respectful, take only photos and leave only footprints.

Granted, the very presence of humans is a form of pollution—no matter how far a hiker rambles he can't get away from himself, can never know *perfect* wilderness. Recently accusations have become common that anyone who encourages enjoyment of trails is engaged in a plot to destroy wilderness. Poppycock! Such accusations are absurd so long as only a small fraction of Northwest wilderness has statutory guarantees and the rest is wide-open to machine-riding predators. In a better future the production of guidebooks may be outlawed and wildness maximized through a conspiracy of silence. In the bad present, however, the need is to put more pedestrians into logger-threatened forests, dammer-threatened valleys, miner-threatened meadows. To be sure, boots violate virginity, but at the moment the alternatives for many a wilderness are more mild punishment by boots or a gang-rape by machines.

Merely to hike is not to contribute to the saving. Each person who through use of this book gains a single memorable day in the back country hereby is put on notice he is expected to repay the debt by joining a conservation organization and begin leaning on the United States Congress to quintuple dedicated wilderness in Northwest states and on the Canada Parliament to increase British Columbia and Alberta preserves by a factor of at least 50. When these goals have been reached it will be time enough to talk about the burning of guidebooks.

Meanwhile, we hope the following pages will bring happy hours to our fellow pedestrians—and will stimulate them to go home afterward and raise hell (unlike the motorized population that wants the wilderness to raise hell *in*).

Ira Spring
Harvey Manning

PLANNING AND NAVIGATION AIDS

MAPS

The first requirement for getting around the country obviously is a set of road maps, either those sold by oil companies or state and province tourist bureaus or contained in a highway atlas.

Most American national parks and monuments and Canadian national and provincial parks offer free information leaflet-maps. With few exceptions these are helpful for broad orientation and road travel but inadequate for hiking.

Though some areas are covered by specialized, privately-published maps which are very useful, the basic tools for wilderness navigation are topographic maps, where they exist, and where not (United States only), maps produced by the U.S. Forest Service.

Topographic Maps

To find the proper sheets for any given trip a hiker must do a bit of homework.

United States

The U.S. Geological Survey (USGS) has prepared topographic maps for most of the nation and is working on the rest. Mountain shops and map stores often stock the sheets for their particular regions, as do information centers in national parks. However, a hiker planning to journey afar usually does best to order direct from:

Distribution Section
U.S. Geological Survey
Federal Center
Denver, Colorado 80225

First ask for an index map (free) of the desired state and from it determine the specific sheets required. An area may be mapped in either or both of two series: the 15-minute series, on a scale of 1 inch to 1 mile; the 7½-minute series, at 2½ inches to 1 mile.

Canada

Topographic maps for British Columbia and western Alberta may be obtained from:
Geographic Division
B.C. Lands Service
Parliament Building
Victoria, British Columbia

Again, first ask for the index map. Some areas are mapped only on a rather unhelpful scale of 1 inch to 8 miles and others on a very good scale of 1 inch to 1 mile. Maps exist for all national parks (except the newest) and most provincial parks.

U.S. Forest Service

Detailed maps are available for a number of wilderness areas and sometimes are topographic; these *wilderness maps*, though not up to high standards of the USGS and often quite confusing, are adequate for ordinary purposes. Most national forests have planimetric *forest maps* or *ranger district maps* which lack contour lines but serve well enough—as they must for places with no other coverage. Those on a scale of ½ inch to 1 mile are best.

Forest Service maps may be obtained from ranger stations, forest headquarters, and the regional headquarters listed below.

Wyoming (most of it)
U.S. Forest Service
Rocky Mountain Region 2
11177 W. 8th Avenue
Box 25127
Lakewood, Colorado 80225

Montana (all) and Idaho (Selway-Bitterroot) Wilderness)
U.S. Forest Service
Northern Region 1
Federal Building
Missoula, Montana 59807

Idaho (most of it) and Wyoming (Bridger Wilderness and Teton Wilderness)
U.S. Forest Service
Intermountain Region 4
324 25th Street
Ogden, Utah 84401

Northern California
U.S. Forest Service
California Region 5
630 Sansome Street
San Francisco, California 94111

Oregon and Washington
U.S. Forest Service
Pacific Northwest Region 6
P.O. Box 3623
319 S.W. Pine Street
Portland, Oregon 97208

Other Maps (with information not elsewhere available)

Oregon (Steens Mountain)
Bureau of Land Management
P.O. Box 2965
Portland, Oregon 97208

Washington (pictorial relief map of the North Central Cascades—Alpine Lakes area)
Recreational Equipment Inc.
1525 11th Avenue
Seattle, Washington 98122

GUIDEBOOKS

Other guidebooks of supplementary value, often considerable, are on the market, and new volumes are being published all the time, but those mentioned in the text are the basic ones for wilderness travel as of 1981. Large mountain shops and some bookstores carry many; if unavailable there, they may be ordered from the sources below.

Wyoming

Orrin Bonney's field guides
Field Book, The Teton Range and the Gros Ventre Range
Field Book, The Wind River Range
Field Book, Yellowstone Park and the Absaroka Range
Field Book, The Big Horn Range
Guide to the Wyoming Mountains and Wilderness (a large volume combining the first four books)
   Swallow Press
   811 W. Junior Terrace
   Chicago, Illinois 60613

Climber's Guide to the Tetons
Teton Trails
   Grand Teton Natural History Association
   Moose, Wyoming 83012

Hiking the Yellowstone Backcountry by Orville E. Bach, Jr.
Hiking the Teton Backcountry by Paul Lawrence
Climbing and Hiking in the Wind River Mountains by Joe Kelsey
   Sierra Club Books
   530 Bush Street
   San Francisco, California 94108

Yellowstone Trails
   Yellowstone Natural History Association
   Yellowstone National Park
   Wyoming 82190

Wyoming Hiking Trails by Sanse and Tom Sudduth
   Pruett Publishing Company
   Boulder, Colorado 80301

Wind River Trails by Finis Mitchell
   Wasatch Publishers, Inc.
   Salt Lake City, Utah 84122

Montana

Rhule's Guide to Glacier (hiking guide to the national park)

Climber's Guide to Glacier National Park
Hiker's Guide to Glacier National Park
   Glacier National History Association
   West Glacier, Montana 59936

Hiker's Guide to Montana
   Falcon Press
   P.O. Box 731
   Helena, Montana 59601

Idaho

Trails of the Sawtooth and White Cloud Mountains by Margaret Fuller
   Signpost Books
   1812 192nd S.W.
   Edmonds, Washington 98020

Sawtooth National Recreation Area by Luther Linkhart
   Wilderness Press
   2440 Bancroft Way
   Berkeley, California 94704

Northern California

41 Hiking Trails of Northwest California by Don Lowe
   The Touchstone Press
   P.O. Box 81
   Beaverton, Oregon 97005

Lassen Volcanic National Park by Jeffrey Schaffer
Marble Mountain Wilderness by David Green
The Pacific Crest Trail, Volume 1 by Jeffrey Schaffer
   Wilderness Press
   2440 Bancroft Way
   Berkeley, California 94704

Oregon

60 Hiking Trails, Northern Oregon Cascades by Don Lowe
62 Hiking Trails, Central Oregon Cascades by Don Lowe
35 Hiking Trails, Columbia River Gorge by Don Lowe
   The Touchstone Press
   P.O. Box 81
   Beaverton, Oregon 97005

Pacific Crest Trail, Volume 2 by Jeffrey Schaffer
   Wilderness Press
   2440 Bancroft Way
   Berkeley, California 94704

Trails of Badger Creek by Ken and Ruth Love
  Signpost Books
  8912 192nd S.W.
  Edmonds, Washington 98020

Guide to the Kalmiopsis Wilderness
  U.S. Forest Service
  Grants Pass, Oregon 97526

Exploring Oregon's Wild Areas
  by William L. Sullivan
  The Mountaineers
  306 2nd Ave. West
  Seattle, Washington 98119

Washington

50 Hikes in Mount Rainier National Park by Ira
  Spring and Harvey Manning
100 Hikes in the North Cascades by Ira Spring and
  Harvey Manning
100 Hikes in the Alpine Lakes by Ira Spring and
  Harvey Manning
100 Hikes in the South Cascades, and Olympics by
  Ira Spring and Harvey Manning
Climber's Guide to the Olympic Mountains by
  Olympic Mountain Rescue
*Cascade Alpine Guide: Climbing and High
  Routes* by Fred Beckey
Volume 1, Columbia River to Stevens Pass
Volume 2, Stevens Pass to Rainy Pass
Volume 3, Rainy Pass to Fraser River
  The Mountaineers
  306 2nd Ave. West
  Seattle, Washington 98119

Stehekin: The Enchanted Valley by Dr. Fred
  Darvill
  Signpost Books
  8912 192nd S.W.
  Edmonds, Washington 98020

Pacific Crest Trail, Volume 2 by Jeffrey
  Schaffer
  Wilderness Press
  2440 Bancroft Way
  Berkeley, California 94704

British Columbia and Western Alberta

*94 Hikes in the Canadian Rockies: Jasper,
  Yoho, and Robson Parks, and Willmore
  Wilderness* by Vicky Spring and Dee Urbick

103 Hikes in Southwestern British Columbia by
  Mary and David Macaree
Exploring Purcell Wilderness by Anne
  Edwards, Patrick Morrow and Arthur
  Twomey
Exploring Manning Park by Robert Cyca and
  Andrew Harcombe
  The Mountaineers
  306 2nd Ave. West
  Seattle, Washington 98119
  co-published in Canada by
  Douglas & McIntyre, Ltd.
  1615 Venables Street
  Vancouver, British Columbia V5L 2H1

Exploring Garibaldi Park by Dan Bowers
  Douglas & McIntyre, Ltd.
  1615 Venables Street
  Vancouver, British Columbia V5L 2H1

The West Coast Trail and Nitinat Lakes
  Sierra Club of British Columbia
  Box 385
  West Vancouver, British Columbia
  V6C 2N2

Alpine Guide to Southwestern British Columbia
  by Dick Culbert
  Alpine Guide
  Box 91402
  West Vancouver, British Columbia
  V7V 3P1

*Climber's Guide to the Coastal Ranges of
  British Columbia* by Dick Culbert
  Alpine Club of Canada
  P.O. Box 1026
  Banff, Alberta T0L 0C0
*Climber's Guide to the Interior Ranges of
  British Columbia* by William L. Putnam
*Climber's Guide to the Rocky Mountains of
  Canada, South* by William L. Putnam
*Climber's Guide to the Rocky Mountains of
  Canada, North* by William L. Putnam
  American Alpine Club
  113 East 90th Street
  New York, New York 10028
Canadian Rockies Trail Guide by Byron Patton
  and Bart Robinson
  Devil's Head Press, Ltd.
  P.O. Box 125
  Canmore, Alberta T0L 0M0

RULES AND REGULATIONS

The very notion of bureaucratic rules and regulations may seem antithetical to the wilderness concept, and certainly is repugnant to those who specifically seek to escape constraints of civilization. However, increases in American population and leisure time, and deterioration in the quality of urban life, have so crowded the back country that perfect freedom rarely is to be found anymore.

To be sure, there still are areas where one may get completely away from Big Brother. But one man's freedom is another's license and in these "free" wildlands the hiker is likely to have his peace disturbed by jeeps and trailbikes, or 100-horse packtrains turning gardens into barnyards, or a regiment of hunters gunning down every creature that stirs, or a pack of yapping dogs, or helicopters flopping from the sky. Even fastidious walkers, if there are enough of them, trample flowers to dust, jam favored campsites elbow to elbow, pollute the waters, and anger the bears.

Land managers responsible for protecting the wilderness owe their first loyalty to the land. If this sounds anti-humanistic, it must be remembered that if the land does not live, which is to say if the native plants and animals do not thrive and the waters do not remain pure, people will have no reason to go there. In future, the freedom of the hills will be limited not only by natural law but human law—which hopefully will sit as lightly as possible.

The problem is relatively new in the Northwest but is worsening rapidly. Managers are seeking solutions, debating which are best, experimenting with techniques. They do not pretend to know the final answers, which must come from trial and error, and they welcome the comments and suggestions of individual travelers.

The permit system (wilderness permit, camping permit, travel permit, fire permit, climbing permit, or whatever) is well-established in most parks and many wildernesses. In some places it is presently employed solely to gather statistics; in others, to regulate the number of visitors and the trails and camps they use, even to the extent of requiring reservations made perhaps weeks or months in advance. Here and there in America a hiker actually may be barred from the trail of his choice, informed it is "full" and he must wait his turn or choose another walk.

The parks are deploying steadily more back-country rangers and the wildernesses more wilderness rangers who observe travel patterns and counsel visitors. In certain areas they have gone beyond the "study and advice" stage and, distasteful as it is to them, have been compelled to act as enforcers, handing out citations for illegal camping and other offenses.

Managers by and large are trying to avoid premature, officious over-control and generally are moving slowly, warily into the era of regulation. Obviously, one way to head off stricter controls, including computerized rationing, is to dedicate more parks and wilderness, and any hiker restive under restrictions surely ought to devote himself vigorously to this cause.

Meanwhile, in his wanderings through the Northwest he will encounter every degree of regulation from none at all to a rigidity which forbids him to camp where he desires, limits his stay to a specified period, requires him to abstain from wood fires and so forth. In any given area, the rules may change from one year to the next. In at least one wilderness, permits were required in 1972 and not in 1973, it having been decided the system was not yet needed there. In at least one national park, campers were concentrated at a few designated sites to confine the damage—and after a short time this policy was junked in favor of the "scattering" technique.

The situation is so fluid the prudent hiker will want to write the appropriate land-managing agency in advance of a trip to learn the current rules and regulations; those published in a guidebook may be obsolete before the ink is dry.

The other thing the hiker can do, aside from obeying existing rules whether he likes them or not, is to comment to back-country and wilderness rangers encountered, and by letter to superintendents of national parks and supervisors of national forests. Though their first loyalty is to the land, they want also to serve the people as best they can, and to do so must know what the people want.

Wyoming

(Above) Deer in the South Wyoming Range
(Opposite) Rappelling in Grand Teton National Park, Teewinot Mountain in distance

Air view of the Absaroka Range on Yellowstone National Park's eastern border

WYOMING

1. Wind River Range (Bridger and Fitzpatrick Wildernesses, and Popo Agie Primitive Area)
2. Gros Ventre Range – proposed wilderness
3. Grand Teton National Park
4. Teton Wilderness
5. Absaroka Range (North Absaroka and Washakie Wildernesses)
6. Yellowstone National Park
7. Bighorn Mountains (Cloud Peak Wilderness)

Other Wildernesses (not described)
8. Medicine Bow
9. Savage Run

Other Wilderness Study Areas
A. Sheep Mountain
B. Snowy Range
C. Laramie Peak
D. Southern Wyoming Range
E. Palisades Back Country

A person looking at a map and noting Wyoming's remoteness from the megalopolis structure of America would expect the wildlands to be virtually empty. Two factors render the situation otherwise. For one, the fault-block ranges of the Rocky Mountain Cordillera rearing dramatically up from the Great Plains are two days' drive closer to Chicago, say, than the Cascades or Sierra and thus for masses of Easterners are among the easiest to reach of high mountains. For another, the scenery ranks with the finest in the West; no peak on the continent is more famous than the Grand Teton; the "gates of hell" in Yellowstone earned it status as the first national park.

Still, though Wyoming suffers some of the worst tourist mobs and some of the fullest trails, large portions of the back country are as purely lonesome as can be found in the old 48.

The land is high, much of it very high, with thin air that makes the miles long. Forests are generally open, broken by broad parks. Tundras glow with flowers in season. Lakes are bright in ice-scooped rock bowls. Summer weather is mainly fair except for the legendary thunderstorms, themselves worth a visit to see. All in all, Wyoming is a hiker's dream.

As for the climber, he scarcely needs to be told the Tetons and Wind River Mountains provide classic alpine tours on the best of rock, offering every degree of difficulty from simple scrambles to experts only.

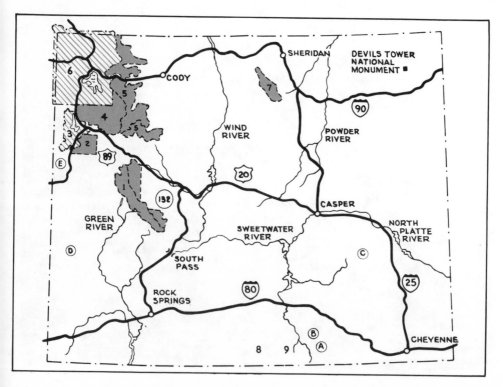

Requiring brief notice here, because it will not be described elsewhere, is Devils Tower National Monument in the northeast corner of the state. The monument is small and thoroughly cut up with roads, but a 1¼-mile trail circles the base of Devils Tower, a volcanic neck which measures 1280 feet from base to top and has been climbed several hundred times.

Clear Creek in the Bridger Wilderness of Wyoming's Wind River Range

WIND RIVER RANGE

(BRIDGER AND FITZPATRICK
WILDERNESSES, AND POPO AGIE
PRIMITIVE AREA)

Administered by Bridger–Teton and Shoshone
National Forests
Wilderness permit required
Best season–July through October
Hiking–excellent
Climbing–excellent
Trail map–Bridger Wilderness map (Pinedale
District)
Guidebooks — **Bonney's Guides, Wind River**
Trails, Climbing and Hiking in the Wind
River Mountains

The Wind River Range offers cold streams flowing through parkland, hundreds of high lakes and miles of tundras and moraines, and 63 living glaciers (including the seven biggest in the Rocky Mountains) covering 44.5 square kilometers, the largest mass of ice in the old 48 states outside the Cascades. And countless granite peaks provide sport for scrambler and climber alike. Topping it all is the highest summit in Wyoming, 13,804-foot Gannett Peak.

A paradise it is for climbers and hikers, and for fishermen too. With 518,500 visitor-days in 1979 this is one of the most crowded wildernesses in the Rockies.

The Bridger Wilderness is located along the Continental Divide. Access is from US 187 and centers on Pinedale on the west. The east portion of the range and approaches from that side lie in the Wind River Indian Reservation (Shoshone and Arapahoe), currently closed to the public.

Fitzpatrick Wilderness is most easily entered from Dubois on US 287.

Seven special management areas of Bridger Wilderness have the following restrictions from July 1 to September 10 to help protect the wilderness resources: groups not to exceed 10 persons; pack and saddle stock not to exceed 20; no open campfires; no camping within sight of any lake or designated trail if within 200 feet; no grazing within ¼ mile of any lake.

Hiking

Hikers unacclimatized to high elevations quickly will learn Wind River miles are twice as long as in lower ranges; itineraries must be planned with this in mind.

Island Lake is among the loveliest in the area and should be seen by every hiker at least once, even though it is mobbed, as are all the lakes with trails. From the Elkhart entrance, 8860 feet, the route climbs gently in 15 miles to the 10,650-foot lake passing several tarns on the way.

Clear Lake has no maintained trail and thus fewer people, yet is easy to find. Start at 7900 feet on the trail that follows the northeast side of Lower Green River Lake; take the left fork up Clear Creek. Formal tread ends in 5½ miles at Natural Bridge. A sketchy path ascends the wooded valley to the 9100-foot lake, 8 miles from the road.

Lonesome Lake, in the southeast portion of the wilderness, is reached by a 10-mile hike from 9100-foot Big Sandy Campground. The trail goes up Big Sandy Creek to Big Sandy Lake, crosses the Continental Divide through 10,600-foot Big Sandy Pass, and drops to (not so) Lonesome Lake at 10,187 feet in the Cirque of the Towers.

Climbing

Ice axes are needed on most peaks in early season but later only on those with glaciers and permanent snowfields. Crampons often are required by summer's end—though the glaciers are

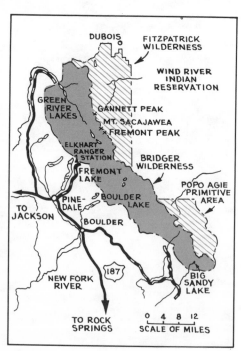

small, much hard ice is exposed. Splendid climbs are so numerous only the highest is noted here. A good many virgin routes still await the expert.

Gannett Peak, 13,804 feet, offers a pleasant combination of ice and rock. Access is very difficult from the west. The easiest approach, which is not so easy, is on the northeast from either Terry Lake or Dinwoody Lake. The trails from these lakes join to follow Upper Dinwoody Creek. Both have considerable ups and downs, dangerous fords in early summer, and require two days to reach the base of the peak. Most climbers, having invested this much time and effort, stay long enough to ascend neighboring peaks such as 13,730-foot Fremont and 13,607-foot Sacajawea.

Hiking Season

Trails are snowcovered through early July. Many of the higher lakes are not clear of ice before mid-July, some not until August. Since the range acts as a cloud-catcher, weather is somewhat wetter than in the rest of Wyoming. Summer typically has a few rainy spells and frequent brief thundershowers. Often there is a stormy week around Labor Day, followed by a clear and lovely Indian summer.

Lonesome Lake and Cirque of the Towers

GROS VENTRE RANGE

Administered by Bridger-Teton National Forest
Best season – mid-June to mid-September
Hiking – excellent
Climbing – very little
Trail map – Bridger-Teton National Forest
  (Teton Division)
Guidebook – Bonney's Guides

Hiking Season

Hiking usually starts in mid-June, only a few snowpatches then remaining to be crossed, but fording streams may be a problem until mid-July. The coming of the hunters in mid-September discourages hikers.

Weather is mainly fair in June, July, and August, though a high percentage of days get afternoon thundershowers.

The Gros Ventre (pronounced grow vaunt) Range is a homey collection of cliffs and gentle ridges, forest patches and large alpine meadows, and open valleys coursed by cold, clear streams. Having few lakes to draw crowds, the area is lightly traveled despite proximity to the superfamous Tetons. The exception is the fall hunting season when hordes of hunters arrive on horseback. Conservationists want the roadless area designated a wilderness.

Located on the south and east sides of Jackson Hole, not the least attraction of the Gros Ventre is marvelous views of the Tetons. One trail starts on the outskirts of the town of Jackson; others are reached from the Gros Ventre River on the north and Hoback River on the south. Elevations run from 7000 feet to 11,750-foot Doubletop Peak. Moose and elk are seen frequently by quiet walkers.

Hiking

The 110 miles of trails (heavily horse-pounded and thus full of loose rocks and protruding roots, and in some cases poorly marked and occasionally hard to find) follow most of the major drainages and lend themselves nicely to three-five-day loop trips as well as day hikes. Many more miles of cross-country rambles invite the experienced wildlander.

All trails lead to great views. Granite Creek on the south side perhaps has a slight edge because of the road-end hot spring—after a tough day one can soak aching muscles in the outdoor hot swimming pool (for a fee).

Climbing

Most peaks are walk-ups, few having any attraction for climbers; some cliffs deserve attention.

Moose grazing along
Granite Creek trail

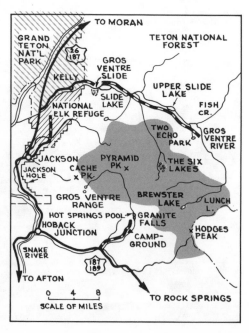

GRAND TETON NATIONAL PARK

Administered by Grand Teton National Park
Camping permit required
Best season—mid-July through September
Hiking—excellent
Climbing—excellent
Trail map—the handout recreation map is inadequate for hikers
Guidebooks—Teton Trails, Climber's Guide to the Tetons, Alpenglow Climbing Guide, and Bonney's Guides

The Teton fault scarp is probably the best-known hunk of rock in America, gaped at by 3,000,000 tourists annually. More and more are getting out of their cars, too, the 134,000 hikers of 1979 doubling the trail population of 1967. Even the summits are mobbed, more than 5000 climbers a summer elbow-jostling in a very small group of peaks.

The popularity is fully deserved. Though trails are loaded with hikers and horses and on "name" peaks climbers must wait in line to get by tough spots, and though gaining privacy for more than a few minutes is virtually impossible, the magnificence makes it all worthwhile, for a brief pilgrimage at least.

All trails and climbs are readily accessible from US 187 in Jackson Hole.

Hiking

Camping permits are required for overnight trips. Space must be reserved in advance at high-country camps. Wood fires are prohibited except at designated lakeshore sites.

When tired of elbows, visit the sparsely-traveled north and south portions of the park, or the West Teton Proposal (see Idaho), or the Teton Wilderness. Or try October.

Lake Solitude. Lots of beauty but no solitude—on an average day 100-200 people walk here, in company with a couple dozen horses which give the path an overwhelming aroma. Cross 6779-foot Jenny Lake by motor launch, then hike to Hidden Falls (there leaving behind the tourist mass) and pick up the Cascade Canyon trail, a fork of which leads in 7½ miles from the boat landing to Lake Solitude, 9024 feet, seldom melted clear of ice until late July. The trail continues 2½ miles to Paintbrush Divide and, in season, one of the best flower fields in the park.

Marion Lake-Death Canyon Loop. Few people here, in the south of the park. The hike starts at 6850-foot Whitegrass Ranger Station, passes above Phelps Lake and proceeds 9 miles through a U-shaped valley, then climbs a 9500-foot pass, contours the west side of Spearhead Peak, re-crosses the ridge, and drops to Marion Lake at 11½ miles, 9240 feet, a good campsite. The loop can be completed by following the Open Canyon trail back to the car, crossing 9210-foot Mt. Hunt Divide. Total distance 25 miles. Generally open in early July.

Climbing

Permits are required for off-trail travel; no restrictions are imposed but rangers like to keep track of folks they might have to find.

Teton Park is the home of the Exum Mountain Guide Service and School of American Mountain-

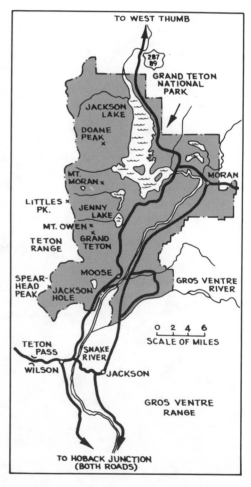

eering. The school quickly (in a day or two) gives flatlanders a smattering of alpine skills, enough to be led up local peaks. The guides supply all special equipment but prefer customers to have their own shoes and insist they have their own clothing.

The Grand Teton offers routes strictly for experts, such as the north face and the north ridge, climbed several times a year. The most popular route is the Exum, not a cinch and with horrendous exposure. Hard hat and two ropes are needed, plus ice ax in early season. The ascent takes two days, the first spent hiking to Garnet Canyon and scrambling to high camp at 11,200 feet in the saddle between Middle and Grand Teton. The second day begins before dawn in order to be off the heights before the typical afternoon lightning storm. Wall Street is the start of the real exposure; from there good but steep rock leads to the 13,770-foot summit. Descent customarily is via the Owen route, easier and gentler overall but with a rappel of more than 100 feet, the reason for two ropes.

Teewinot Mountain. Less experienced climbers may find this 12,325-foot peak sufficient and surely will feel well-rewarded, not only by the rockwork but the close-up views of 12,928-foot Mt. Owen and the awesome north face of the Grand. Ice axes are always handy and a necessity early in the season. Rope is optional but may be wanted. For the most pleasant trip, hike the 4½-mile trail from 6750-foot Lupine Meadows to Amphitheater Lake, 9700 feet, and camp overnight. Next day follow the trail to the edge of the Teton Glacier, ascend the ice, then scramble to the summit.

Hiking Season

High trails don't melt out until mid-July and are likely to be snowed in by late October. June is often rainy, as is the last week of August. The rest of the summer is generally fair except for afternoon thunder and lightning. September may be the best hiking month of all.

Camp near Lake Solitude, Grand Teton in background

TETON WILDERNESS

Administered by Bridger-Teton National Forest
Best season – late July through early September
Hiking – good
Climbing – none
Trail map – Teton Wilderness
Guidebook – Bonney's Guides

The Teton Wilderness is big enough to get lost in, if a person is so inclined. A land of rolling hills and 12,000-foot peaks, the western third wooded, the eastern two-thirds largely barren ridges and vast meadows brilliant with flowers in late July and August; many marshes and at times an ungodly number of insects. Around the east edge, a generous scattering of petrified wood, leaf molds, and shell fossils. The most famous feature is Two Ocean Creek, which runs along the Continental Divide a way, then splits into Pacific Creek and Atlantic Creek, each ultimately feeding a separate sea.

Located in the headwaters of the Yellowstone and Snake Rivers, the wilderness is bordered on the north by Yellowstone National Park, on the west by Grand Teton National Park, and on the east by Washakie Wilderness. The only easy access is on the south from US 26/287.

Hiking

Numerous dude ranches use this wildland for elaborate pack trips so a hiker may be forced to dodge strings of up to 50 horses. Since in summer the horse people gang up around the few fishing-type lakes, a true wilderness experience can then be enjoyed by avoiding lakes, and especially by leaving the trail. However, during hunting season, from September 10 through October, the country thuds with hooves and bangs with guns, the cavalry attack led by commercial outfitters.

Much of the area is made impossibly wild for hikers in spring and early summer by never-bridged streams raging with snowmelt. Only after late July can a pedestrian hope to safely cross the big ones. The difficult fords are on Atlantic Creek, the Yellowstone River at Woodward Creek, North and South Buffalo Creeks, and Thorofare Creek.

South Buffalo Fork Creek. Start from 7000-foot Turpin Meadow, reached from US 26 about 8 miles east of Grand Teton National Park. The trail (which has many ups and downs) can be hiked in early July since the lower crossings of the creek are bridged. On a day walk or backpack, see grand displays of wildflowers in July, or in September perhaps moose.

Two Ocean Loop. A lot of miles and days are needed to get properly into the spirit of the Teton Wilderness. This 80-mile loop, minimum recommended hiking time 10 days, does the job best. Begin at Turpin Meadow on North Buffalo Fork trail, go up Soda Fork past Crater Lake, over the Continental Divide, drop into Woodward Canyon, and follow the Yellowstone River down to Yellowstone Meadows. Ascend Atlantic Creek to recross the Continental Divide at 8200-foot Two Ocean Pass, where Two Ocean Creek splits. Descend Pacific Creek to Enos Lake, then cross a low divide to North Buffalo Fork for the return to Turpin Meadow.

Climbing

Every mountain can be walked up.

Hiking Season

Trails are usually snowfree (if not floodfree) by the end of June and stay open through October. July and August are mostly fair, averaging about a day of rain a week. July is pretty buggy. September and October actually have the best weather, and though it's the only season bears are a major problem, hikers then may see moose and elk; unfortunately, this is hunting season.

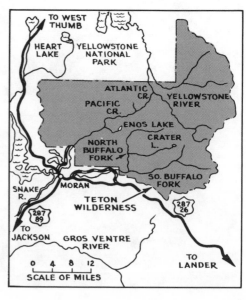

North Buffalo Fork River

ABSAROKA RANGE

(NORTH ABSAROKA AND WASHAKIE
WILDERNESSES)

*Administered by Shoshone National Forest and
   Yellowstone National Park*
Camping permit required in the park portion
Best season–July through October
Hiking–good
Climbing–poor
*Trail map–Shoshone National Forest recrea-
   tion map (little help to hikers)*
*Guidebooks–Bonney's Guides; Recreation
   Opportunity Guide may be read and copied
   at ranger stations*

A long, high range, mostly of crumbling volcanic rock with a bit of rotten granite thrown in for
variety, sculpted by glaciers and streams into deep,
narrow canyons, bright-colored pinnacles and
cliffs, and broad, meadow-crested ridges. The
wildland is busy in the fall, when horseback
hunters travel in strings of 50 or more animals, but
the rest of the year the scenery is viewed by very
few people riding or walking.

The range extends from Montana through the
east side of Yellowstone National Park and ends
just north of Jackson Hole. The mountains lie in
the park, the Absaroka-Beartooth Wilderness (in
Montana), North Absaroka Wilderness, Washakie
Wilderness, and Teton Wilderness. The
best access is from Cody on the east side of Yellowstone
National Park, driving either the Sunlight Creek
road or the South Fork Shoshone River road.

Hiking

This is prime country for the loneliness of the
long-distance walker; though there are one or two
good short hikes, most are 50 to 80 miles. Trails
are well-maintained and clearly signed, but
bridges are few and fords are dangerous during
snowmelt, generally until mid-July. During flood-
time boulders big enough to break a hiker's leg can
be heard rumbling down the streams.

For a day walk which can stretch into a week,
try the Boulder Basin trail, which starts at South
Fork Ranger Station and in 5 miles climbs 2600
feet to 9000 feet on Boulder Ridge and aerial views
of the South Fork valley. Parties with three or four
days can continue on, roaming meadowland and
easy ridgetops. Water may be scarce up high.

South Fork Shoshone River. A 22-mile round
trip to the mouth of Needle Creek provides views of
open meadows, waterfalls, and wildlife, notably
bighorn sheep. From just west of Cody drive the
South Fork road about 40 miles to either of two
trailheads (both about 6500 feet), at Majo Ranch
or South Fork Ranger Station; the latter approach
is 2 miles longer (13 miles one way) but saves
fording the river. At the ford the two approach
paths unite in a single trail which, with many ups
and downs, follows the valley, sometimes climbing
500 feet above the river, then dropping again.

Yellowstone River Loop. An 85-mile trip. Starts
on the South Fork Shoshone trail, ascends Marston
Creek to Marston Pass on the Continental Divide,
there entering Teton Wilderness. Descend the
Yellowstone River to Bridger Lake, climb Thorofare Creek to Deer Creek Pass, then drop 4000 feet
down Deer Creek to the South Fork road.

Lamar Valley. This 60-mile loop offers fine
opportunities to see elk, bighorn sheep, and
buffalo. Begin at 7000-foot Crandall Ranger
Station on the Cody-Cooke City road. Go up North
Fork Crandall Creek to the Yellowstone Park
boundary, down Cache Creek trail to Lamar River,
up the valley to Miller Creek, on up to Bootjack
Gap, and finally down Hoodoo Creek to the start-

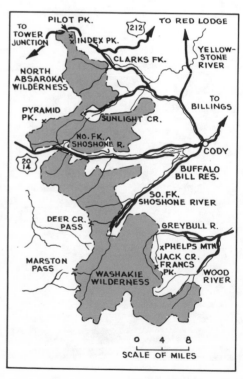

ing point. Camping permit is required for the section in the park.

Climbing

The mountains are either simple walks or climbers' nightmares, the cliffs often beautifully colored but so loose the handholds are largely portable and even the wind triggers rockfalls. All summits have been attained, of course, but the difficult routes are too rotten to attract experts. However, a couple of easy peaks rise above timberline and offer superb panoramas.

Francs Peak, 13,140 feet. This peak has not only views but a chance to see elk and sheep. From Meeteetse, on State Highway 120, drive up the Greybull River, then the Jack Creek road to the end—the last 4-5 miles are rough, barely negotiable by an ordinary car. Ascend 4500 feet from the road-end. No trail but no problems—just proceed up.

Windy Mountain, 10,275 feet, a lookout site and thus with a summit trail. From 16 miles north of Cody on Highway 120 drive Sunlight Basin road to the winter game range. The trail goes up Painter Creek, climbing 3000 feet in 5 miles.

Hiking Season

Trails are generally snowfree from mid-June to late October, but trails involving river fords aren't passable to hikers until late July. From mid-June to mid-September skies are mostly clear except for occasional afternoon thundershowers, usually real drenchers when they come. It's a rare summer without a week of continuous bad weather bringing a few inches of snow.

Absaroka Range and Sunlight Creek valley

YELLOWSTONE NATIONAL PARK

Administered by Yellowstone National Park
Camping permit required
Best season—July to mid-October
Hiking—good
Climbing—poor
Trail map—the handout map is inadequate for hiking
Guidebooks—Hiking the Yellowstone Backcountry, Yellowstone Trails, Bonney's Guides

A paradox: Yellowstone is among the most popular of the national parks, yet for those able to put one foot in front of the other, offers unlimited solitude. The park occupies a high, wooded, volcanic plateau, or group of plateaus, at an average elevation of 8000 feet, crossed by the Continental Divide and surrounded by mountains —the Absaroka Range on the east, the Gallatin and Madison Ranges on the west, and the Tetons on the south. Though the 500 miles of roads are thronged by millions of tourists, 95 percent of the park's 3500 square miles is lonesome back country with uncrowded geyser basins, rolling alpine meadows, and forests both living and petrified.

Hiking

The several hundred miles of trails, mainly built by the army in the 19th century, were laid out to get horse patrols from one place to another as quickly as possible. No thought was given to the recreational hiker, who came along years later, and therefore most routes go viewless miles through lodgepole pine and many involve river fords easy enough for horses but difficult for pedestrians. Which is not to complain—these very features guarantee the peace and quiet a wildland roamer seeks.

Camping permits, required for all overnight hikes, are issued at park ranger stations within 48 hours of a trip. Demand is very high for a few popular camps but obtaining permits is no problem for most of the park. If planning a trip in the back country, be sure to ask rangers about current bear reports.

Mt. Sheridan. A panoramic view of the park from the 10,308-foot summit and, on the way, a wonderful wilderness lake, hot springs, and a small geyser. The trail starts near Lewis Lake at 7800 feet, gently climbs 400 feet in 4 miles to hot springs and a viewpoint of Heart Lake, then descends through forest and past more hot springs to good campsites at 7450-foot Heart Lake, 8 miles. West along the lakeshore ½ mile is Rustic Geyser, a fountain erupting approximately every half-hour. The Mt. Sheridan trail leaves the lake near the geyser and switchbacks to the fire lookout atop the peak and broad views of lakes, miles and miles of unbroken forest, and the distant Tetons. In season the crest is covered with tiny arctic flowers.

Mt. Washburn. Park at the Chittenden road barricade and hike the 3½-mile trail to the fire lookout on the 10,243-foot summit. The trail provides a glorious view and an opportunity to get a close look at the bighorn sheep which make the mountain their summer home. In season, lovely flower fields line the first mile of the trail, which starts at 8839-foot Dunraven Pass and follows a long-abandoned road up the peak.

Shoshone Geyser Basin. An outstanding thermal area reached by an easy 8-mile trail from the Lone Star Geyser road, or by canoe from Lewis Lake up the Lewis River (some pulling required in shallow water) and then across Shoshone Lake. No powerboats are allowed on the river or lake. Afternoons often are too windy for paddling, so start early.

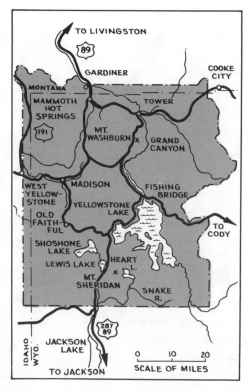

Specimen Ridge trail goes over the top of 9614-foot Amethyst Mountain and passes near two petrified forests; some trees are still standing. In early July the lovely bitterroot blooms on rocky knolls, succeeded by other blossoms in the week or two before the ridge dries up. Views over plains of Lamar Valley and into Yellowstone Canyon. The trail begins a few miles east of Tower Junction at 6200 feet, climbs steeply for 3 miles, then wanders several miles along the crest to Amethyst Mountain. The petrified trees are difficult to find; ask the ranger-naturalist at Tower Junction for directions.

Climbing

Most peaks of the Absaroka Range, which crosses the northeast corner of the park, have easy sides. Many have spectacular faces but are of such rotten rock serious climbers rarely are interested.

Hiking Season

The high country is generally snowbound until early July and buried again in late October. Weather is mostly fair from July through September. Bugs are very bad in early summer, especially just after the snow melts.

Lewis River near Shoshone Lake

BIGHORN MOUNTAINS

(CLOUD PEAK WILDERNESS)

Administered by Bighorn National Forest
Best season – July through September
Hiking – excellent
Climbing – good, what there is of it
Trail maps – Bighorn National Forest recreation
map (poor for hikers), Bighorn National
Forest (a charge, if available)
Guidebooks – Bonney's Guides

The Bighorns are a lofty range, 120 miles long and 30-50 miles wide, lifting abruptly from 4000 feet in the Great Plains to a 7500-9000-foot plateau, above which peaks stand another 3000-4000 feet. The mountain scarp (known locally as The Face) rises dramatically from plains and ranches on every side except the south; the tallness and the deep slicing by colorful canyons are very striking.

The plateau is mainly rolling hills of forest and meadow. The central part is thoroughly dissected by logging roads and jeep tracks. A few trails remain unwrecked in the north but most hiking is in the south, in the Cloud Peak Wilderness, a magnificent area of granite cliffs, tundra, and numerous alpine lakes.

The Bighorns, located well east of the Continental Divide, are crossed by US 14, connecting Greybull and Sheridan. The easiest access to the wilderness is from US 16 at Meadowlark Lake, driving an excellent forest road to West Tensleep Lake.

Hiking

The range is popular both with horsemen and and hikers. As is true everywhere in the West, the fish in timberline lakes are the major attraction; Cliff Lake, Solitude Lake, Geneva Lake, and Seven Brothers Lakes are especially crowded. For privacy one does well to carry a stove and camp above timberline and distant from fishing.

The wilderness paths receive minimal maintenance and only the main loop trail (see below) is signed. Open ridges invite off-trail roaming and the experienced navigator can do any number of superb cross-country journeys. However, the thin air makes the miles longer than in lower ranges, a fact to be remembered when planning trips.

Cloud Peak Loop. Peaks of the wilderness are completely circled by a fairly well-maintained loop trail of about 60 miles, with only moderate ups and downs. The main trail and major junctions are signed, but not the spurs; on side-trips the map must be carefully watched. Many starting points are possible, Big Goose Creek being the easiest. To reach the trailhead, drive US 87 about 5 miles south of Sheridan; at a mile short of Big Goose Ranger Station turn onto Big Horn-Little Goose Creek road, and soon turn up Big Goose Creek road to its end. The loop goes over Geneva Pass, past Lake Solitude, over Florence Pass, near Seven Brothers Lakes, out around a ridge to Hepp Cow Camp, up Kearney Creek to Highland Park Lakes, and finally back to the Big Goose Creek road.

Mistymoon Lake gives a nice view of the glaciated cliffs of Cloud Peak and provides a good jump-off for hikes to Lake Solitude and for cross-country ramblings. From the road-end at 9100-foot West Tensleep Lake, the trail passes Lake Helen and Lake Marion and at 5½ miles joins the Cloud Peak Loop trail at 10,200-foot Mistymoon Lake.

To escape horses, try Lost Twin Lakes, in a wide semicircle of ice-plucked cliffs 6 miles from West Tensleep Lake. The trail starts fine but soon becomes too rough for the cavalry.

Some canyons outside the wilderness provide interesting hikes, including Devils Creek, Wolf Creek, Tongue Creek, Little Horn Creek, and possibly Goose Creek. Trails are sketchy or

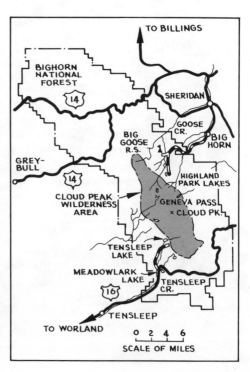

absent. Other canyons are either too cliffy or end in private property. Watch for rattlesnakes.

Climbing

The notable peaks all are in the wilderness. Though most are walk-ups, a few spires and northeast faces deserve the attention of cragsmen and one major summit cannot be attained without alpine skills.

Blacktooth, 13,014 feet, second-highest peak in the range, is the remnant of a basalt dike standing on a granite base. Every route requires ropes, hardware, hard hats, and experience. The approach is from Spear Lake.

Cloud Peak, 13,165 feet, the climax of the Bighorns, is a hiker's mountain, though at times an ice ax can be handy. The approach is from Lake Solitude or Mistymoon Lake. An unmaintained, unsigned trail leads to the top and memorable views of the entire range, the Great Plains, and in the mind's eye, scenes of such battles as the 1876 wipe-out of Custer's command by the Sioux.

Hiking Season

The country is high and snow stays late, comes early. Trails are generally open from about the first of July to the end of September. Weather during this period is fair except for frequent afternoon thunderstorms—but about once a summer the range gets a week of rain.

Mistymoon Lake and Cloud Peak, from the Cloud Peak Loop trail

Montana

(Above) Bighorn sheep grazing near the Garden Wall, Glacier National Park
(Below) Air view of the Chinese Wall, Bob Marshall Wilderness

Mt. Wilbur and Swiftcurrent Lake, Glacier National Park

MONTANA

1. Madison Range (Spanish Peaks Wilderness
   Management Area, and Hilgard and Lionhead–proposed wildernesses)
2. Hyalite Peaks–proposed wilderness
3. Absaroka-Beartooth Wilderness
4. Crazy Mountain–proposed wilderness
5. Anaconda-Pintler Wilderness
6. Gates of the Mountains Wilderness
7. Bob Marshall, Great Bear, and Scapegoat
   Wildernesses
8. Mission Mountains Wilderness
9. Jewel Basin Hiking Area
10. Glacier National Park
11. Cabinet Mountains Wilderness

Other Wildernesses (not described)
12. Welcome Creek
13. Rattlesnake
14. Red Rock Lakes

Other Wilderness Study Areas
A. West Big Hole
B. Barb and Maurice Mountains
C. Middle Mountain, Tobacco Roots
D. Flint Range
E. Hoodoo
F. Tuchuck

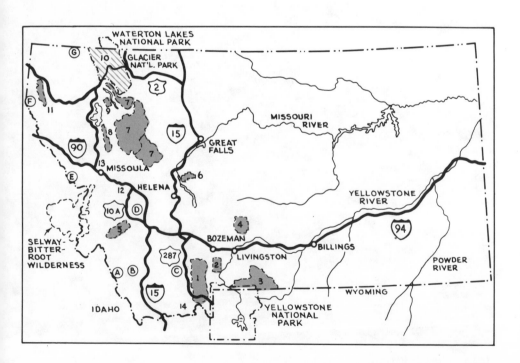

Few experiences of the American earth are as thrilling as traveling westward in Big Sky country of the Great Plains, horizons unending in all directions, and suddenly realizing the line of high clouds looming ahead is the Rocky Mountains. The entirety of western Montana consists of various ranges of the Rockies, which extend south into Wyoming, west into Idaho and north into Canada.

The mountains are mainly for hikers, with thousands of miles of delightful trails at elevations from 3000 to 11,000 feet. In the more easterly ranges forests begin to thin at about 8000 feet and few trees grow above 10,000; the corresponding elevations are roughly 1500-2500 feet lower in the western part of the state. Some 106 small glaciers totaling 10 square miles are scattered in half a dozen ranges. One of the handful of summits that cannot be attained by walking or scrambling is 12,799-foot Granite Peak, Montana's highest. However, rock-climbers find numerous ice-plucked east and north faces of every degree of difficulty, the rock varying from solid granite to sedimentary and volcanic crud. The weather through June is often very wet and cold; July and August and the first half of September are generally fair except for afternoon thunderstorms.

Until the past generation, Montana was one great wildland, disrupted only here and there by residents, who with certain notorious exceptions blended almost Indian-like into the landscape. In the 1930s the great Bob Marshall and a few compatriots led the way toward gaining official dedication of some portions as wilderness, but there really seemed little danger much of the back country would ever be radically altered. Now, however, the citizens of Montana are confronted by a proliferation of roads, off-road vehicles, and developers appropriating large areas for super-resorts. Conservationists thus are pressing a number of proposals for new dedicated wildernesses. Some of these are tremendously complicated by the checkerboard ownership dating from the infamous Northern Pacific Land Grant—a problem also nagging Idaho and Washington.

Trail to Grinnell Glacier, Glacier National Park

MADISON RANGE

(SPANISH PEAKS WILDERNESS MAN-
AGEMENT AREA, AND HILGARD AND
LIONHEAD—PROPOSED WILDERNESSES)

*Administered by Gallatin and Beaverhead Na-
tional Forests*
*Wilderness permit required for Spanish Peaks
only*
Best season—late June through September
Hiking—good
Climbing—little
*Trail maps—Gallatin National Forest Recrea-
tion Map (inadequate for hikers), Gallatin Na-
tional Forest Travel Plan Map, Spanish Peaks*
Guidebook—Hiker's Guide to Montana

The Madison Range, west of Yellowstone National Park between the Madison and Gallatin
Rivers, runs 60 miles from Idaho north nearly to
Bozeman. Though highways give enticing views
of the peaks, the mountains are ignored by the
swarms driving to Yellowstone and Grand Teton
National Parks. The alpine lakes are used heavily
and a few of the many trails are pounded by dude-
ranch packtrains but there is lots of solitude.

The proposed wilderness of the southern or
Lionhead section, cut off from the rest of the range
by the Madison River Canyon (site of Earthquake
Lake, formed by a giant earthslide in 1959), lies on
the Continental Divide and contains several summits over 10,000 feet and numerous lakes.

The climax is the proposed Hilgard Wilderness,
north of the Madison River Canyon, with miles of
beautiful meadows, a few lakes, and good-looking
peaks rising above 11,000 feet.

The northernmost section is a bit less impressive, though with at least one peak above 11,000
feet, but often is preferred by hikers because it
centers on the machine-free Spanish Peaks Wilderness Management Area.

Until jeeps and trailbikes are cleaned out, the
ranges west of the Madisons—Gravelly Range,
Tobacco Root Mountains, Pioneer Mountains, and
others—cannot be enthusiastically recommended
despite their beauty.

The Madison Range is reached from US 191
between West Yellowstone and Bozeman.

Hiking

Lionhead. The alpine lakes are accessible by
an 8-10-mile trail from Highway 87 north of
Henrys Lake.

Hilgard. The best access is the Beaver Creek
road from Earthquake Lake. Three trails start at
7000 feet on Beaver Creek and ascend to broad
gardens so glorious in July it is worth putting on
bugproof clothing and a headnet and braving
mosquitoes too numerous to be discouraged by
repellent alone.

The first trail leads 6 miles to Blue Danube and
Avalanche Lakes. The second climbs 7 miles up
Sentinel Creek to 10,100-foot Expedition Pass;
a sketchy path below the pass goes over a low ridge
into Hilgard Basin and its cluster of small lakes
beneath 11,214-foot Echo Peak; an easy cross-
country route from the basin over another ridge
attains more lakes under 11,316-foot Hilgard

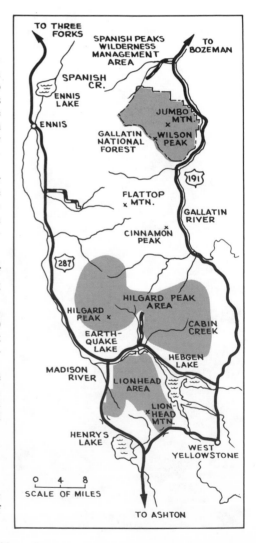

Peak. The third trail goes 4 miles to Lightning Pass, then through meadows to 9401-foot Moose Butte.

Another good trip is 10 miles from Red Canyon to rolling tundra between Sage Peak and White Peak.

Spanish Peaks Wilderness Management Area. From US 191 a steep path leads to Table Mountain, a shorter one to Lava Lake. The best hike, ordinarily very private, is from the road-end at 6000-foot Spanish Creek Camp, reached from US 191 south of Bozeman, up South Fork Spanish Creek. Walk the main valley, then try any of the tributaries—all culminate in meadows at 8000-9000 feet.

Climbing

Though the peaks are sharpened by ice and some require considerable scrambling, not much of the sedimentary, schistose, and gneissic rock is attractive to climbers, beautiful though it is to look at.

Hiking Season

Trails are usually free enough of snow for hiking by the end of June. Winter often closes the country in October. June weather is generally wet, early July has frequent thunderstorms, and late July and all of August are mainly clear, and often September too.

Insects are fierce in Lionhead and Hilgard meadows, mosquitoes in July and trillions of black flies in August. September has no bugs but many hunters.

Hilgard and Dutchman Peaks from Beaver Creek trail

HYALITE PEAKS

Administered by Gallatin National Forest
Best season—July to mid-October
Hiking—excellent
Climbing—none
Trail maps—Gallatin National Forest Recrea-
    tion Map (inadequate for hikers), Gallatin
    National Forest Travel Plan Map
Guidebook—Hiker's Guide to Montana

The Hyalite Peaks, at the north end of the Gallatin Range, form the southern horizon of Bozeman, with 12 mountains (largely of volcanic rock) over 10,000 feet, 20 spectacular waterfalls, numerous meadows, a few lakes in cirque basins, and classic examples of U-shaped valleys. The Porcupine-Buffalo area to the south contains part of the Gallatin Petrified Forest. Checkerboard ownership makes wilderness classification difficult, but without it private resorts doubtless will be built on Burlington Northern Railroad land. The alpine beauty of the Bridger Range north of Bozeman also deserves protection.

Hiking

Hyalite Mountain is a joyful hike. Drive the Hyalite Reservoir road south of Bozeman to its end. The trail gains 3200 feet, starting with 3 miles in forest, passing innumerable waterfalls, at 5½ miles reaching 8800-foot Hyalite Lake, surrounded by flower fields, and at 7½ miles the 10,299-foot summit and panoramas of mountains and the Yellowstone River. In early July a difficult river crossing at 4 miles, below Apex Falls, can be bypassed by not making the crossing but rather climbing the east bank of the falls to a long-abandoned yet very decent trail. Also at that season, a hiker will feel better with an ice ax while climbing steep snow near the top of the peak.

Climbing

All mountains are walk-ups.

Hiking Season

Hyalite trails are snowfree from mid-July to early October. The best time is when enough snow remains to stop motorcycles and horses. The flowers climax after the snow has melted. Summer weather is mostly clear with occasional thundershowers.

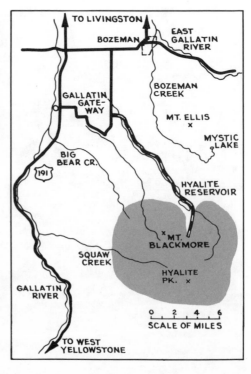

West Fork Hyalite Creek valley

ABSAROKA-BEARTOOTH WILDERNESS

Administered by Custer and Gallatin National Forests
Best season—mid-July to October
Hiking—excellent
Climbing—good
Trail maps—Gallatin National Forest Travel Plan Map, Custer National Forest Map
Guidebook—Hiker's Guide to Montana

Absaroka-Beartooth Wilderness is the rooftop of Montana, with 12,799-foot Granite Peak, highest in the state, 25 other summits above 12,000, 10 sky-open plateaus of an average elevation greater than 11,000 feet, 40 glaciers, 300 lakes, 5000 waterfalls, enormous tundras, and deep, forested, U-shaped valleys. Rocks are a complex mixture of sediments, granite, and volcanics. Ghost towns from old mining days are scattered on the Boulder River side.

The wilderness lies along the boundary of Yellowstone National Park. Access is easy from US 212, which crosses 10,945-foot Beartooth Pass between Cooke City and Red Lodge. The northeast portion can be reached by the Boulder River road from Big Timber, south of Livingston on US 89, a jeep road from Cooke City, or in Yellowstone National Park to Silvertip Ranch.

Hiking

The problem is choosing where to go; splendid trails are many, only a few really crowded, and the cross-country rambling is unsurpassed in the Northwest. The thin air, of course, slows the pace.

Trail No. 570. A fine introductory sampling. It starts at beautiful Island Lake, 9600 feet, near Beartooth Pass on US 212, and stays high past numerous lakes and meadows to 9800-foot Green Lake. The trail ends at 14 miles but more lakes invite further exploration; the return trip could be done along trail-less ridges or by trail-less lakes.

East Fork Rosebud Creek. The most popular hike, beginning from the 8200-foot road-end and touching lakes, lakes, and more lakes, including, at 10 miles, Lake At Falls, named for the cataract tumbling into tranquil waters. The path crosses a 10,000-foot divide near Fossil Lake and at 32 miles reaches US 212 just 4 miles from Cooke City.

Grasshopper Glacier. About 200 years ago a horde of migrating grasshoppers (locusts) suffered icing problems in a storm, crashed to earth, and were entombed in the snow. Only a few specimens from that doomed flight are left, many having melted out and decomposed in a 1919 hot spell, but every year more grasshoppers fall from the sky so chances of finding some are good, especially at the glacier snout. (The phenomenon is common in the Rockies and several other glaciers have the same name, including those in the Wind River Range and the Crazy Mountains.) The glacier is located 11 miles from US 212 near Cooke City. Since 9 of these miles are on an abandoned mining road passable to jeeps, the best bet is to rent a jeep in Cooke City, leaving only a 2-mile hike, gaining about 800 feet, to the edge of the glacier at 11,000 feet.

Eastern Absaroka. Trails are gentle and with few exceptions lightly traveled, open forests permit easy cross-country roaming, and water is fairly accessible—all in all, a great area to get away from people.

Climbing

Granite Peak, 12,799 feet. There is no easy way to the top and the northeast face ranks as one of the great walls of Montana. The standard route (requiring ice ax and rope) starts at the 6400-foot end of the West Rosebud road. From high camp at 11,500 feet near Froze to Death Mountain ascend to a saddle between Granite and Tempest Mountain, continue up the east face of Granite to the crest of the first ridge, go out on the north face, back around to the south face, and up to the summit.

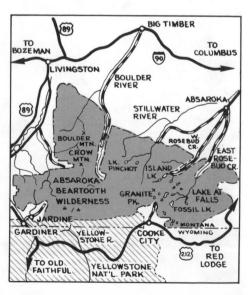

One of the most spectacular mountains visible from Granite is 11,489-foot Wolf Peak. The east face has a small but vigorous glacier.

Pilot Peak, 11,740 feet. Famous because tourists see nothing from highways of the region to match its drama. Actually it lies in the Absaroka Wilderness of Wyoming but due to proximity is best noted here. Soaring above US 212 near Cooke City, Pilot and its companion, Index Peak, are the remains of a volcano. Though the ascent is not technically difficult the rock is horribly rotten. The route to the 11,000-foot saddle between the two peaks is a lovely hike, starting at about 7200 feet and following a faint trail up Index Creek. Having enjoyed the walk, climbers can then decide whether they wish to dare the dangers of the crumbling cliffs.

Hiking Season

The area is so high and cold the season starts late and ends early. Many trails are not snowfree until mid-July and some lakes are frozen well into August. A heavy snowfall may come in mid-September but paths usually are passable to mid-October. Summer weather is mainly good except for rather frequent thunderstorms, which in the bare highlands can be very scary.

Pilot Peak near Cooke City

CRAZY MOUNTAINS

Administered by Gallatin and Lewis and Clark National Forests
Best season – July and August
Hiking – fair
Climbing – some
Trail maps – Gallatin National Forest Recreation Map (inadequate for hikers), Gallatin National Forest Travel Plan Map, and Lewis and Clark National Forest Travel Plan Map
Guidebook – Hiker's Guide to Montana

The Crazies in South Central Montana often are the first real mountains an Easterner traveling westward over the Great Plains ever has seen in his whole life. Though a small range, barely 15 by 20 miles, the granite fault block stands as an impressive, isolated island rising from 4000-foot prairies to green forests and snowy summits culminating in 11,214-foot Crazy Peak. In the alpine back country, so far known and visited by few people, are meadows, small cirque lakes, and three glaciers.

As the story goes, a woman in an emigrant wagon train went insane, escaped custody, and was found near the base of the range — thereafter called Crazy Woman Mountains, then Crazy Mountains, and commonly referred to as the Crazies.

The Crazies deserve and demand wilderness status. However, the ridiculous and corrupt Northern Pacific Land Grant continues to visit sins of the 19th century on the present. The Forest Service says the checkerboard ownership rules out any chance of wilderness. Conservationists say otherwise, and never mind that heirs of the Big Steal have other plans. Though the private land makes temporary difficulties for the public, it is also true that the intermixed public land can be defended in such a way as to permanently forbid private exploitation.

The range is seen from Interstate 90 at Big Timber and along US 191 between Big Timber and Harlowton. Access is awkward because most roads to the national forest boundary cross private land and the public as yet has not gained (rather say, re-established) legal right of passage. The only sure way is the Big Timber Canyon road, and since much of it is not graveled access is far from sure in wet weather.

Hiking

From Big Timber drive 12 miles north on US 191, then up Big Timber Canyon road to the end at about 6000 feet. (Some of the finest views of the Crazies are from this road before it enters the canyon.) The trail starts at a locked gate near Half Moon Campground and follows the river 4½ miles to Twin Lakes. Granite, Pear, and Thunder Lakes can be reached by cross-country travel.

Climbing

All peaks have walk-up or scrambling sides but Crazy, Granite, and Conical present attractive north and east faces of solid granite. Mountain goats often are companions of climbers.

Hiking Season

Trails are sufficiently snowfree for walking from June through October but muddy roads make July and August the only safe months. Summer weather is generally dry except for occasional thunderstorms.

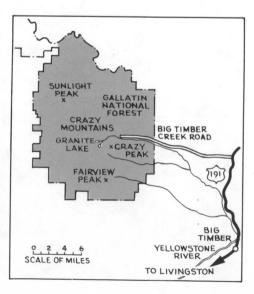

Bitterroot, Montana's state flower, blooms in early summer

Crazy Peak from Big Timber Canyon road

ANACONDA-PINTLER WILDERNESS

*Administered by Deerlodge, Bitterroot, and
    Beaverhead National Forests*
Best season – July through September
Hiking – fair
Climbing – very little
Trail map – Anaconda-Pintler Wilderness
Guidebook – Hiker's Guide to Montana

Forests and meadows, cirque lakes and craggy peaks, U-shaped valleys and deep canyons in a wilderness astride 30 miles of the Continental Divide. Elevations vary from 5000 feet to 10,793-foot West Goat Peak. The granite center is flanked by sedimentary rocks. The name comes from the Anaconda Range, which here forms the Continental Divide, and Charles Pintler, an early trapper and settler who made this country his home.

The area is lively, but short trails to countless alpine lakes plus a large number of commercial packers add up to many, many people and many, many horses.

Roads ring the wilderness. Most trails are reached from US 10 alternate between Anaconda and Philipsburg.

Hiking

Johnson Lake. Though all the lakes are busy, Johnson Lake, an easy two-hour walk, attracts so many people that camping has been prohibited. From Highway 38 drive Moose Lake road to its end at about 6000 feet. The trail leads in 4 miles to the 7720-foot lake.

Warren Lake. More miles and thus more privacy. Accessible by trails from any of three forest roads from Highway 43. All the trails start at about 6000 feet and in some 15 miles reach 8462-foot Warren Lake, set in a cirque surrounded by high peaks.

Climbing

Most summits are scrambles but some granite faces are interesting.

Hiking Season

Though snowfall is rather heavy, trails are usually open enough for walking in early July and not blocked again until mid-October. High lakes often are frozen until mid-July. Summer months are more sunny than wet but there may be extended spells of rain in July and September; August has occasional thunderstorms.

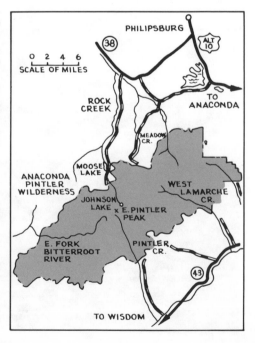

September snow at Johnson Lake

GATES OF THE
MOUNTAINS WILDERNESS

Administered by Helena National Forest
Best season – mid-June through October
Hiking – good
Climbing – none
Trail map – Gates of the Mountains
Guidebook – Hiker's Guide to Montana

A small wilderness (6 by 9 miles) in the Big Belt Mountains, this range of rolling limestone hills is dissected into impressive canyons and minaret-like spires. Vegetation varies from steppe grasses and shrubs along 3600-foot banks of the Missouri River (14 inches of annual precipitation) to a forest starting at 5000-6000 feet (25 inches) to subalpine trees and plants on the nearly 8000-foot ridgetops.

On July 19, 1805, Meriwether Lewis, following the Missouri upstream, named its canyon through the west edge of the Big Belt Mountains the "Gates of the Rocky Mountains." A reservoir now floods the canyon but the weird cliffs and the Lewis and Clark campsite are still there. In the 1940s Duncan Moyr, Supervisor of Helena National Forest, initiated a one-man crusade to preserve some of the Big Belts — most of which are crisscrossed by roads and motorbike trails. By 1948, he was successful.

The two entries to the wilderness, one by boat and the other by car, are easily reached from Helena. From Memorial Day to Labor Day a tour boat leaves Upper Holter Lake daily at 10 a.m. and 2 p.m. The Figure 8 road leads to the trailhead at Refrigerator Canyon. The jeep roads to other trails are not recommended.

Hiking

The wilderness is pounded hard during hunting season but is virtually empty in summer, what with no lakes to draw mobs, just scenery. The main attractions are the canyons, Meriwether and Willow being the best.

Water is a problem. Willow Creek is the only dependable stream, others often flowing underground. A ranger can mark a map with locations of the scattered springs. Rattlesnakes are too few to be a major nuisance.

An 18-mile trail traverses the wilderness and many of its highlights. Experienced hikers can take a side-trip from the middle of the traverse up

7100-foot Willow Mountain — an unmarked, unmaintained fire trail circles around the north side of the peak to the top, which offers tremendous views of the spires and canyon below. If a one-way walk is planned, shuttle transportation must be arranged.

For the western approach to the traverse, drive Highway 16 (Interstate 15) north from Helena, take the Gates of the Wilderness exit to Upper Holter Lake, and board the tour boat. Have the pilot let you off at Meriwether Campground, then hike up Meriwether Canyon, the trail steeply climbing 2500 feet, passing a lovely meadow near Kennedy Springs.

For the eastern approach, drive from Helena to Hauser Lake and continue to the village of York, where Figure 8 road splits. Both forks lead to the trailhead at Refrigerator Canyon; the left fork is a bit shorter but the right fork up Trout Creek Canyon and over Hogback Mountain is by far the most exciting.

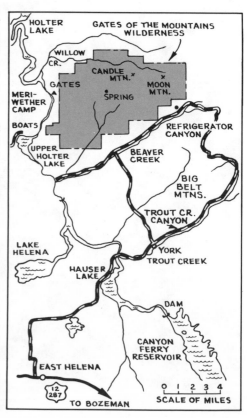

Climbing

Challenging as the spires are, climbing on the crumbling limestone is unthinkable.

Hiking Season

Trails are snowfree about mid-June, an es-pecially good time for a visit since meadows are still green and alive with flowers. The country often stays open through November. Weather from June to mid-September is usually hot and dry except for lightning storms once or twice a week.

Refrigerator Canyon

BOB MARSHALL, GREAT BEAR, AND SCAPEGOAT WILDERNESSES

Administered by Flathead, Lewis and Clark, Helena, and Lolo National Forests
Best season—June through October
Hiking—good
Climbing—none
Trail maps—Bob Marshall Wilderness, Scapegoat Wilderness
Guidebook—Hiker's Guide to Montana

This huge wilderness is famed for miles and miles and miles of forested ridges and bright, clear rivers. The excitement lies in the vastness of far-from-civilization back country rather than in eye-opening scenery, though here and there the sedimentary rocks have been ice-sculptured to striking cliffs of vari-colored strata. The climax is the Chinese Wall, a huge overthrust forming the Continental Divide for a great distance, the crest at an elevation of 8000-9000 feet, the west side a gentle meadow slope, and the east a precipice 200-300 feet high unbroken for some 25 miles and indeed resembling the Great Wall of China.

Because of the long trails, the wilderness traditionally has been the special domain of horse-riders and is surrounded by busy commercial packers; paved landing strips are located near trailheads for fly-in "dudes." However, pedestrians are claiming their share and in 1970 for the first time outnumbered equestrians.

The Bob Marshall Wilderness was named for one of the chief saints of the American wilderness movement, personally responsible for millions of acres of the national forests being saved from multiple use. It and the newer (1978) supplement, the Great Bear Wilderness, are located along the Continental Divide just south of Glacier National Park, reached on the north from US 2 and Hungry Horse Reservoir, on the west from Highway 209, and on the east from US 89.

Years of persistence by local conservationists, supported by national groups, were rewarded in 1972 by establishment of the Scapegoat Wilderness, the first area in the nation lacking previous administrative protection to be placed in the National Wilderness Preservation System. The preserve is too small, however, and the effort thus must continue. Similar in character to the Bob Marshall Wilderness it neighbors on the south, Scapegoat Wilderness trails are acces-

sible from several forest roads from Highway 20 near Lincoln.

Hiking

The east side of the wildland probably is best for a first taste of its subtle pleasures, the country being a bit more open and the scenery more varied than on the west—even though the west-side Swan Range nourishes the area's one glacier.

The main trails (South Fork Flathead River, Salmon River to Big Salmon Lake, White River, and South Fork Sun River) are wide, dirty, and much-thudded by packtrains. Hikers should leave them for side-trails, and a better chance of solitude, at first opportunity. Since only the very tops of ridges extend above timberline, cross-country travel is difficult.

Gordon Pass. An easy sampling of the southwest corner of the Bob Marshall Wilderness. From Highway 209 drive to the Holland Lake Recreation Area parking lot at about 4000 feet. Hike 6 miles to Upper Holland Lake and 2 miles more to 6500-foot Gordon Pass on the wilderness boundary. Several

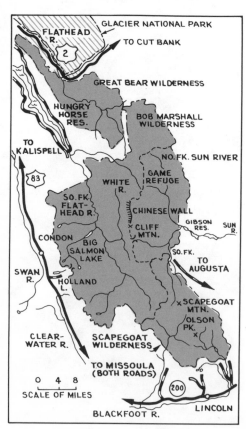

small lakes on the far side of the pass invite camping and exploring.

Chinese Wall via Indian Point. A 26-mile route (or 17-mile variant) to the famous spectacle, the way passing through broad valleys of lodgepole pine with frequent openings for views. From Highway 287 at Augusta drive the Benchmark recreation road 29 miles to the 5000-foot road-end at the edge of Sun River Game Refuge. The trail descends South Fork Sun River 5½ miles, entering the wilderness at 4½ miles, then ascends the West Branch of the South Fork, forests broken by numerous small parks, to Indian Point at 12 miles. Here the trail splits, one fork going up Indian Creek to the Chinese Wall in 5 miles. The other fork, much longer and more scenic, climbs in timber 5 miles to meadows on the slopes of Cliff Mountain. A side-trip to the 8500-foot summit gives a close and impressive look at the Chinese Wall.

Climbing
   Forget it.

Hiking Season
   Lower trails are snowfree in early June, higher trails by the end of the month. Hikers have the most fun when a good sprinkling of snowdrifts remains, stopping horses and providing plentiful drinking water. Trails often are passable through October. Summer weather is generally sunny, with occasional extended spells of rain and a certain number of thunderstorms.

Carmine Peak from trail near Upper Holland Lake

MISSION MOUNTAINS WILDERNESS

Administered by Flathead National Forest
Best season–late June through October
Hiking–good
Climbing–little
Trail map–Mission Mountains Wilderness
*Guidebook–**Hiker's Guide to Montana***

This area is a long, narrow range of wooded hills and tree-ringed valley lakes, rock-bowl alpine lakes in parkland beneath cliffs, and sharp little peaks and small glaciers. The fame of nearby Glacier National Park helps keep the trail traffic down. The west side of the range, which holds some of the most exciting country and the highest point, 9868-foot McDonald Peak (with two glaciers), lies in the Flathead Indian Reservation; hopefully the Indians will preserve their wild heritage.

Mission Mountains Wilderness is located just west of Bob Marshall Wilderness, the two divided by the Swan River valley. The best access is from forest roads off Highway 209 near Condon.

Hiking

Lakes. Beautiful as Turquoise, Glacier, Cold and Frigid Lakes are, they are overused and best avoided except in the offseason—and best visited on day hikes only. For Turquoise, from Highway 209 drive Rusk Creek road 12 miles to the 4900-foot trailhead. Hike 6 miles to the large lake at 6424 feet, on the way climbing above beautiful but impassable buttresses of glacier-carved rock. The lake is nestled under Mt. Shoemaker, which carries a tiny glacier. Make a ¼-mile detour to visit lovely Glacier Lake at 5300 feet. Some years the area is loaded with beargrass in early July.

Cross-country traverse. The classic trip in the Missions entails leaving trails; an ice ax is helpful and a climbing rope useful in case a party strays off the route into cliffs. From Highway 209 drive Beaver Creek road to the 5000-foot trailhead. Hike 8 miles to the trail-end at 6646-foot Gray Wolf Lake. Climb north to a 7800-foot pass, drop to 6311-foot High Park Lake, climb another 7800-foot pass and drop to 6227-foot East Lake, climb a third 7800-foot pass and drop to Turquoise Lake. The off-trail distance is only 6 miles but is rough enough to take most hikers three days—plus two-three days on the trails.

Climbing

Though all peaks have easy sides, many have respectable faces that doubtless will receive more attention as time goes on.

Hiking Season

Trails are usually snowfree in late June, lakes in mid-July. Winter white returns in October. June is wet and cool, July sun is interrupted by occasional thunderstorms, and August is clear and very hot until the last week, when a long rain may begin. The cool and crisp and bright Indian summer of late September and early October is the best of all possible times for a hike.

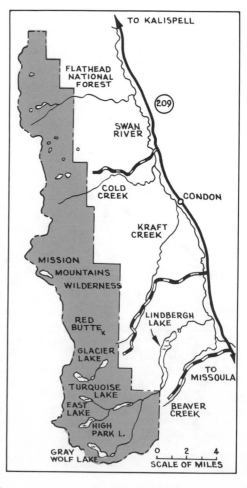

Daughter-of-the-Sun Mountain and Lagoon Lake

JEWEL BASIN HIKING AREA

Administered by Flathead National Forest
Best season—July through October
Hiking—good
Climbing—none
Trail map—Jewel Basin Hiking Area Map
Guidebook—Hiker's Guide to Montana

A small wildland, some 2 by 10 miles, Jewel Basin Hiking Area is at the north end of the Swan Range, mostly wooded but with 28 mountain lakes and a number of little meadows. The highest peak is 7529-foot Mt. Aeneas, whose northwest slopes can be walked to the summit.

The special joy of Jewel Basin is that the Forest Service has designated it for hiking only—despite loud objections from horsemen and motorcyclists. The freedom from conflict has so excited local pedestrians there is no chance of loneliness; this and the small size make the highland best suited for day trips. A larger portion of the Swan Range is proposed for wilderness by conservationists.

Jewel Basin is located between Kalispell and Hungry Horse Basin.

Hiking

The 35 miles of trails connect most of the lakes, several of which have campsites. Except on ridgetops cross-country hiking is difficult.

Of the four entries, the easiest is Noisy Creek road No. 5392 from Highway 83. Several trails from the road-end climb in 2-3 miles to intersect Alpine Trail No. 7, which runs the length of the area close to crests and offers the most interesting hike.

Climbing—None

Hiking Season

Trails usually are snowfree from early July through October. June is generally wet and cold, July and the first half of August clear except for occasional thunderstorms, and the second half of August wet again. September often has a lovely Indian summer with a good show of fall colors.

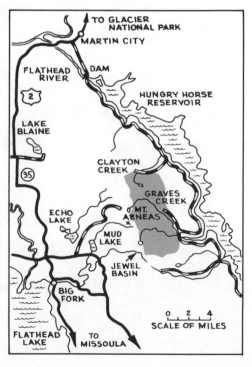

Glacier lilies and Mt. Aeneas

GLACIER NATIONAL PARK

Administered by Glacier National Park
Camping permit required
Best season—mid-July through September
Hiking—excellent
Climbing—fair
Trail map—Waterton-Glacier Backcountry
(inadequate for hikers)
Guidebooks—Hiker's Guide to Glacier National
Park, Climber's Guide to Glacier National
Park, Rhule's Guide

The overwhelming climax of the Continental Divide and the Northern Rockies is Glacier National Park, with hundreds of precipitous peaks of spectacular structures, 53 small glaciers and 200 lakes, gleaming streams and flower-shining meadows, and shadowy forests at elevations as low as 3100 feet—thus making for very *tall* mountains.

The more than 600 miles of maintained trails and another 100 usually passable offer a hiker material for years of explorations. He must, however, be prepared to find his freedom within a framework of restrictions forced by the trail-crowding, perhaps the worst in the Northwest.

With adjoining Waterton Lakes National Park across the border in Canada, the park constitutes the Waterton-Glacier International Peace Park—an example that ought to be followed elsewhere along the 49th Parallel.

Access is from Going-to-the-Sun road over 6664-foot Logan Pass, Swiftcurrent Lake road, a narrow dirt road to Kintla Lake, by tour boat from Waterton Lakes in Canada, and Two Medicine road and Highway 2 on the south and southeast.

Hiking

Before venturing into the back country carefully read the park leaflet, *In Grizzly Country*, and from it learn the rules of "defensive hiking." Also ask rangers about the current bear situation along the planned hiking route.

Camping permits are required, issued first-come, first-served during a two-day period preceding the first night planned on the trail. Reservations are needed for accommodations in hikers' chalets at Granite Park and near Sperry Glacier.

Grinnell Glacier. One of the most rewarding day hikes in the park. Also among the busiest, since ranger-naturalists conduct guided trips. The trail starts at 4875-foot Swiftcurrent Lake, passes beautiful Lake Josephine, and comes close to Grinnell Lake, set in a magnificent cirque. From here the way climbs in earnest, views down to the lakes steadily growing. In 6 miles the trail ends at the 6300-foot edge of Grinnell Glacier.

Gunsight Pass, 6900 feet. Grand views and an almost guaranteed chance to see mountain goats. From 3100-foot Lake McDonald climb to Sperry Chalet at 6½ miles and Gunsight Pass at 10 miles. The pass can be reached from the other side by a 10-mile hike from St. Mary Lake.

Elizabeth Lake-Glenns Lake loop. A six-day loop trip amid some of the park's finest scenery. From Swiftcurrent Lake the trail climbs past Ptarmigan Lake, then high on Ptarmigan Wall, at the top actually tunneling through the wafer-thin crest. The way traverses the shore of Glenns Lake to a camp at Stoney Indian Lake. The fourth night is spent at 50-Mile Camp and the fifth and last at Granite Park Chalet, from where the route climbs over Swiftcurrent Pass to return to the lake.

Climbing

The great walls make climbers drool with anticipation. However, most rock is so unstable that few peaks are ascended except by the easiest routes—and many of these are dangerous. Hard hats are recommended on all peaks and some require rope, ice ax, and crampons.

Clements Mountain, 8764 feet. The dominant

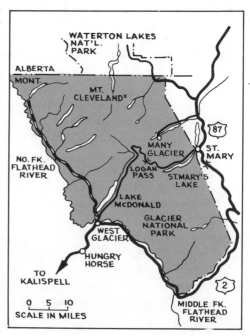

peak of the Logan Pass vicinity. From the pass follow Hidden Lake trail 2½ miles to an elevation of 6800 feet. If the correct series of animal trails can be found, the summit is attained by a moderately-difficult scramble.

Mt. Wilbur, 9293 feet. A startling hunk of rock thrusting above Swiftcurrent Lake, one of the most difficult peaks in the park and requiring considerable rock-climbing experience. Short pitches demand careful belaying—and rappelling gear for the descent. Starting from Swiftcurrent Lake, follow Swiftcurrent Pass trail 2 miles, then ascend into a large snowy cirque and choose between the "overhang route" and the "staircase route."

The climb is normally done in a single very long day.

Hiking Season

Forest trails near Lake McDonald are snowfree in June but high trails usually are impassable until mid-July due to steep and dangerous snowbanks that cannot be bypassed.

June is generally wet, cool, and windy. July and the first three weeks of August are mainly clear and hot with occasional rainy spells and thunderstorms. Snow can begin in late August but the high country ordinarily remains open until early October.

Swiftcurrent Lake and Mt. Gould

CABINET MOUNTAINS WILDERNESS

*Administered by Idaho Panhandle and Kootenai
  National Forests*
Best season—July through mid-October
Hiking—excellent
Climbing—little
Trail map—Cabinet Mountains Wilderness
Guidebook—Hiker's Guide to Montana

Climbing

All peaks have walk-up sides but a few north faces are interesting.

Hiking Season

Low trails usually are snowfree in early June, the high ones in early July. Deep snow can be expected in late October. June weather generally is cold and wet, July and August mostly fair with occasional thunderstorms. Some years September and the first half of October are beautiful but other years are wet.

A slender range drenched by 100 inches of annual precipitation that feed a maritime-type forest of cedar, fir, and hemlock with an understory of huckleberry and devil's club. Elevations run from 2500-3000 feet at road-ends to 8712-foot Snowshoe Peak, timberline being about 7000 feet. Cirque lakes are numerous, their basins carved in sedimentary rock except around Granite Creek; three tiny glaciers survive. Atop summits one looks out over ridge upon ridge of mountains in this northwest corner of Montana, all nearly as high as the Cabinets and once as attractive but now all thoroughly crisscrossed by logging roads.

Cabinet Mountains Wilderness, located several miles from Libby, is reached from US 2 on the east and north sides and Highway 202 on the west.

Hiking

Only 12,000 visitor-days were recorded in 1971 and 95 percent of these by pedestrians, so the trails, though steep, are in fair shape. Vegetation is dense and ridgetops rugged and cross-country travel therefore is not recommended; the lonesome off-trail lakes demand difficult battles.

One of the easiest samplings of the wilderness is the 2-mile hike to Leigh Lake under the towering cliffs and two glaciers of Snowshoe Peak. Don't expect solitude.

At the south end a trail follows the crest of the Cabinet Divide through several miles of an old burn with great views. On the east, the Granite Creek trail leads to alpine lakes.

The most exciting hike is at the north end, where a steep trail climbs 3000 feet in 5 miles to Upper Cedar Lake, continues to the Cabinet Divide, and traverses the crest from Dome Mountain to Sugarloaf Mountain before descending to Flower Creek. A number of sidetrails drop to lakes.

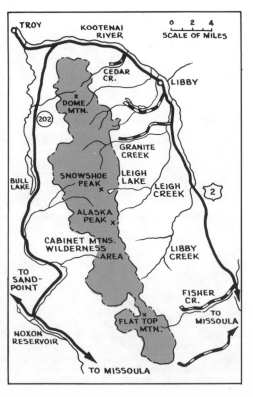

Upper Cedar Lake and Dome Mountain

Idaho

(Above) Hells Canyon, Hells Canyon Wilderness
(Opposite) McGowan Peak, Sawtooth National Recreation Area

Sawtooth Lake and Mt. Regan, Sawtooth National Recreation Area

IDAHO

1. Craters of the Moon National Monument
2. Western Tetons—proposed wilderness
3. Sawtooth Wilderness and Sawtooth National Recreation Area
4. Lost River Range
5. Hells Canyon National Recreation Area— Hells Canyon Wilderness, Seven Devils Scenic Area
6. River of No Return Wilderness
7. Selway-Bitterroot Wilderness
8. Salmo-Priest and Scotchman Peak—proposed wilderness

Other Wildernesses (not described)
9. Gospel Hump

Other Wilderness Study Areas
A. Mt. Naomi
B. Palisades Back Country
C. Italian Peaks
D. Pioneer Mountains
E. Smokey Mountains
F. Lick Creek
G. Patrick Butte Lava Ridge

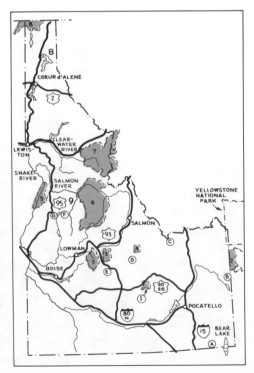

Idaho north of the Snake River plains is one grand maze of mountains, sagebrush-covered on lower slopes, forested from 4000-6000 feet up to 9000-10,000 feet, above that sculptured by Pleistocene glaciers into cliffs and cirques now bare of ice but with summer snowfields and rocky parks and sparkling lakes and flowery meadows. Attractive as are the highlands, the canyons are perhaps even better known—certainly among river-runners.

Until recently the state's wilderness was so vast and empty it was a great place for a person to get so lost nobody could even begin a search. Then came jet-set dude ranches, an uncontrolled invasion by jeeps and the "poor man's horse," the trailbike, and simultaneous movement into the back country by loggers and dammers and big-corporation miners. And lo! It was realized that Idaho is, after all, finite. As a result, some of the nation's hottest wildland battles were fought in the 1970s, and partly won, partly lost (but conservationists will regroup to fight again).

Though some areas no longer are worth walking and others are now crowded, there still is plenty of room for a hiker to be lonesome and enchanted. Except for granite spires of the Sawtooths few peaks challenge expert climbers, but the off-trail scrambler can find good fun everywhere.

Castle Peak, Sawtooth National Recreation Area

CRATERS OF THE MOON NATIONAL MONUMENT

Administered by Craters of the Moon National Monument
Back country use permit required for overnight
Best season—May through October
Hiking—rugged
Climbing—none
Trail map—handout map suffices for short hikes
Guidebook—none

A broad lava field dotted with little spatter cones, large cinder cones, a few lava caves, and tree molds. The 83 square miles of lava include the rough *aa* and the smoother *pahoehoe*.

Though the most recent flow was about 2000 years ago, much of the area appears as barren and sterile as if the rock cooled only yesterday. However, a closer look reveals small flowers in tiny niches and on the older flows vegetation is fairly well established.

US 20/26 passes through the northwest corner of the monument near Arco. Paved roads give access to most of the non-wilderness portion.

Hiking

Nearly all important features can be seen from the road or the five easy nature trails, but a few—lying in the Craters of the Moon Wilderness which comprises more than half the monument—are reserved for the determined hiker.

A two-day, 10-mile exploration leads to the mile-long rift called Vermilion Chasm, at the south edge of the monument. The trip also provides solitude: in 1980 only 342 people took the hike. The route starts from the Tree Molds parking area and follows an abandoned road 4 miles; navigation of the remaining 6 miles is strictly by map and compass. The required permit can be obtained from the Visitors Center.

Heat exhaustion, dehydration, and twisted ankles are the main hazards. Getting lost in a spring or fall fog is another, and being trapped in a lava field during one of the occasional lightning storms can get a bit hairy.

Climbing—None

Hiking Season

July and August are hot and windy. The best times for hiking are May-June and September-

October, but be prepared then for rain and fog. May has the edge because there usually are a few snowpatches for water—the scattering of summer waterholes is badly contaminated by birds and small animals. Water and a stove must be carried. Camping is best on soft cinder areas rather than rough lava.

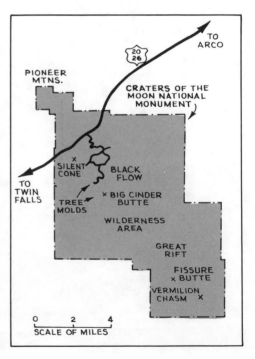

Spatter Cone nature trail

Pahoehoe lava along the Tree Molds trail

WESTERN TETONS

Administered by Targhee National Forest
Best season – July through September
Hiking – excellent
Climbing – some
Trail maps – West Slope Tetons Map, Targhee
  National Forest East Division (½ inch to
  1 mile)
Guidebook – Petzoldt's Teton Trails

The West Slope of the Tetons is unknown to Jackson Hole hordes but the alpine meadows and ridgetop trails are delightful in themselves and offer spectacular views of the great peaks. The sedimentary rock structures, capping underlying granite and quartzite, are tilted, allowing easy ascents of western slopes, then dramatic looks down abrupt eastern cliffs.

How this wonderful portion of so famous a range was omitted from the national park is a mystery. Conservationists now are seeking wilderness status if not addition to the park as well. They are urging further that the Teton Corridor, which separates Teton and Yellowstone National Parks and is threatened by a new highway which would be an ecological disaster, be placed in one park or the other and the existing little road and its surroundings be kept primitive.

Though entirely in Wyoming, the area is included in this book's Idaho chapter since that state provides the easiest access—from Highway 32 near Driggs.

Hiking

National park camping permits, required only for hikers continuing into the park, may be obtained from Forest Service rangers at Driggs. Elsewhere, permits are required only in Alaska Basin.

Alaska Basin. This small group of alpine lakes is the most famous part of the West Slope—and the most crowded. In fact, it is mentioned here to suggest it be avoided except for day hikes. The national forest approach is a long day on a pleasant trail up the South Fork Teton Creek. A side-trip to Devils Stairway is a must—a steep trail around beautiful cliffs and small meadows overlooks Alaska Basin.

Table Mountain. A rough trail climbs 4000 feet in 6 miles from North Fork Teton Creek to the 11,101-foot summit, from whose eastern shoulder one can gaze 1000 feet down into the park's Cascade Creek and across to the 3000-foot west face of Grand Teton.

The most solitude and best scenery are in drainages north and south of Teton Creek, such as to Granite Basin and Green Lakes and up South Fork Badger Creek. A high trail connects all three areas; at many spots one can walk easily to the ridge crest for stunning views of the Tetons.

Climbing

A few east-slope cliffs are of some interest but the sedimentary rock is not up to standards of high-Teton granite. Many climbers approach park peaks from this side.

Hiking Season

Meadows are green and trails generally walkable by early July, though with snowfields lingering and some creek crossings difficult from snowmelt. High trails usually are white by the end of September. Summer weather is the same as in the national parks, which is to say mainly clear with afternoon thunderstorms.

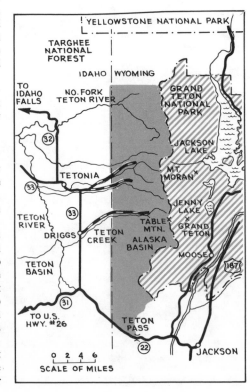

West side of Grand Teton from Table Mountain

SAWTOOTH WILDERNESS AND SAWTOOTH NATIONAL RECREATION AREA

Administered by Sawtooth National Forest
Wilderness permit required
Best season – July through October
Hiking – excellent
Climbing – some
Trail maps – Sawtooth National Forest North Division Recreation Map, Sawtooth Wilderness
Guidebooks – Trails of the Sawtooths and White Cloud Mountains, Sawtooth National Recreation Area

A new national park? That was the hope. In 1972 Congress reclassified the old primitive area as the Sawtooth Wilderness and created an adjoining Sawtooth National Recreation Area. It also directed the U.S. Forest Service to study for wilderness designation undeveloped country in and near the recreation area, specifically the White Cloud Peaks, Boulder Mountains, and Pioneer Mountains. It further directed the National Park Service to study the entire region for potential as a park, the goal conservationists sought. The result of this (first) campaign was — status quo. Except in the dedicated wilderness, trailbikes are permitted to run quite free; an enormous open-pit molybdenum mine still is proposed for the very heart of the White Clouds. Insult to injury, cattle and sheep continue eating the flowers in Sawtooth Wilderness.

The White Cloud Peaks are much the same as the Sawtooths, high and rugged, except that the rock is strikingly-colorful limestone and old volcanics — substantially mineralized, more's the pity.

Highway 75, between Ketchum and Stanley, gives access to (and spectacular views of) the Sawtooths west and White Clouds east. Highway 21 from Boise skirts the west and north sides of the Sawtooths, whose south side is reached by primitive forest roads.

Highway 75, between Ketchum and Stanley, gives access to (and spectacular views of) the Sawtooths west and White Clouds east. Highway 21 from Boise skirts the west and north sides of the Sawtooths, whose south side is reached by primitive forest roads.

Hiking

Sawtooth Wilderness. A grand land for hiking. A good introduction is the easy 4½ miles to Bench Lake, the trail climbing 1000 feet atop a moraine overlooking Redfish Lake. Lots of people, horses, and scenery. The most popular trip is the 5 miles to Sawtooth Lake; enjoy the views but hike a mile farther to McGowan Basin for a bit of privacy.

Of the 180 lakes, the 178 other than mobbed Sawtooth and Bench are hardly touched. Ten Lakes Basin from Atlanta offers a chance of solitude, which is guaranteed at the many lakes without trails, accessible only by cross-country roaming.

White Cloud Peaks. Little Boulder Lakes, a half-dozen alpine lakes in parkland on the north flanks of 11,820-foot Castle Peak, are exactly where the open-pit mine would be located. Approach by driving up East Fork Salmon River and hiking either the Big Boulder or Little Boulder Creek trails, both about 8 miles long and with the same elevation gain. The first 2 miles of the Little Boulder trail pass through hot sagebrush, starting at 6300 feet and climbing 2000 feet to the lakes; the Big Boulder trail starts in forest at 7500 feet, climbs over a 9000-foot pass, then drops to the lakes.

Big Boulder Lakes. A fork of the Big Boulder trail leads in 5 miles to a group of lakes between 8000 and 8500 feet. The basin is pretty but not as spectacular as Little Boulder Lakes.

Climbing

The major Sawtooth peaks all have walking or scrambling sides but the needles and north walls

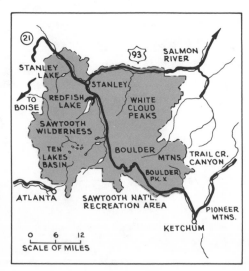

delight rock climbers, who come from far away to enjoy the sport on sound granite under blue skies. The rock of the White Clouds is colorful but too unpredictable for serious climbing.

Hiking Season

Trails are mainly open, with some snowpatches, in mid-July; high lakes may be frozen a month later. Outside the Sawtooth Wilderness June is the best time for hikers, the snow stopping horses and trailbikes. However, mosquitoes then are almost unbearable in spots. Winter snows generally return in October or November.

Weather is good in June and excellent from July to October, sunshine interrupted only by occasional thunderstorms. Once in a while though, an extended rainy spell comes—usually timed for the 4th of July or Labor Day holidays.

Sawtooth Lake and trail to McGowan Basin

LOST RIVER RANGE

Administered by Challis National Forest
Best season—May and June for most areas, July
*   for Borah Peak*
Hiking—fair
Climbing—none
Trail map—Challis National Forest Map
*Guidebook—*Forest Service leaflet, Hiking
*   *Guide for Borah Peak

The highest point in Idaho, 12,655-foot Borah
Peak, is the climax of the Lost River Range,
a long, narrow fault block of sedimentary rock
pushed up between two downdropped blocks
forming valleys. Together with its neighbor
block on the east, the Lemhi Range, it should be
dedicated as wilderness if only to get rid of the
racketing, soil-eroding, animal-harassing jeeps
and motorcycles which in recent years have driven
hikers from lower slopes and most high trails
as well.

Though rather parched in summer, the country
is flower-sprinkled and grassy-green and snow-
patch-scattered and creek-rushing in spring, superb
for walking when snowier mountains of the region
are over the knees in whiteness.

US 93 from Challis to Arco traverses the valley
beneath the Lost River Range on the west. A
partly-paved, partly-gravel road follows the valley
between the Lost River Range and the Lemhi
Range.

Hiking

Borah Peak gives broad views over mountains
and valleys of Idaho and Montana. The summit
can be ascended by trained climbers even in
winter, if weather permits, and May is probably the
most pleasant month for pedestrians accustomed to
snow-plugging and equipped with ice axes. July is
best for ordinary hikers; no special equipment is
needed then except a large sun hat. Don't omit can-
teens, though; snowpatches linger on the route
until July (and on the north side of the peak
most of the summer) but the heat may force
constant drinking.

A well-signed, unmaintained road climbs 2
miles from US 93 to the base of Borah at about
7700 feet. There is no trail, nor is one needed.
Simply climb the sagebrush slope north of the
road-end and follow the west ridge through open

forest, then rocks and tenacious little flowers,
to the summit panorama.

Climbing

All peaks in the Lost River and Lemhi Ranges
can be walked up and the rock is too crumbling
for face-climbing.

Hiking Season

Most of the highland is snowfree in May or
June and the coolness and greenness make this
the best walking time. Snow returns in October
or November. Lightning storms are common in
summer heat and on Borah the first buildup of
towering clouds should be the signal for hasty
retreat.

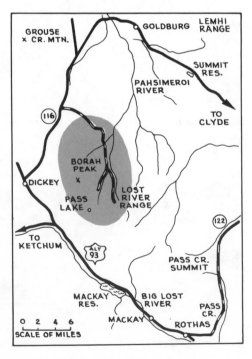

Borah Peak

HELLS CANYON NATIONAL RECREATION AREA

(HELLS CANYON WILDERNESS, SEVEN DEVILS SCENIC AREA)

Administered by Wallowa-Whitman, Nez Perce, and Payette National Forests
Rafting permits required, wilderness permits voluntary
Best season—Seven Devils, July-October; Hells Canyon, March-May and September-October
Hiking—good
Climbing—none
Trail map—none
Guidebook—none

This area features craggy remnants of ancient volcanoes, snowcapped most of the summer, with some 40 cirque lakes set amid subalpine forest of pine, larch, spruce, and fir. Several air miles away and five life zones and 8000 feet below, the Snake River flows through the deepest canyon in the United States, sagebrush and cactus on the rocky banks. The Seven Devils, whose name recalls the long-ago ordeal of a lost Indian brave, are 9393-foot He Devil, the highest, and She Devil, Devils Tooth, Devils Thumb, Tower of Babel, The Ogre, and The Goblin. Lesser peaks have less frightening names. Hells Canyon contains the free-flowing (so far) Snake and myriad memories and artifacts from days of the Indians, explorers, and miners.

The east side of the area is traversed by US 95 south of Grangeville. Hells Canyon can be reached by a very rough forest road to Pittsburg Landing, and the mountains by forest road from Riggins to 7600-foot Seven Devils Campground.

Hiking

Seven Devils. An approximately five-day loop trip around the peaks passes many of the lakes. For a shorter hike, a 3-mile fishermen's path, happily too rough for trailbikes, leads to Mirror Lake, first climbing 600-700 steep feet with a short scramble up a bare cliff to a saddle, then contouring a hillside and descending scree to the lake. Sheep Lake is accessible by the same route.

Hells Canyon. A number of trails drop from the high country 5000-6000 feet into the canyon— easy enough descents but grueling returns, with no timber for shade below 4000 feet. The best plan is to drive to Pittsburg Landing on the Idaho side of the Snake (there is also a trail on the Oregon side) and hike upstream. The trail rarely stays long at river level, constantly rising above cliffs and in the process giving spectacular views. An alternate method is to start at Hells Canyon Dam with a 2-mile boat ride to Lamont Springs, then hike 35 miles downstream to Pittsburg Landing. Boats can be arranged by contacting Jim Zenilli or Ralph Page, outfitters in Oxbow, Oregon. From February through April parts of the trail may be flooded but most such sections can be bypassed.

Climbing

Some cliffs of the Seven Devils are very challenging but the volcanic rock is so extremely rotten few climbers are tempted.

Hiking Season

Snow does not melt from Seven Devils trails until late June and some lakes remain frozen weeks later. Summer months are dry and hot with occasional thunderstorms. Snow usually blocks trails in early November.

Hells Canyon is open much of the year. From June to August temperatures often soar above 100° in the shade—and there isn't any. Early spring is best for hikers; it's usually plenty warm even then. Fall also may be pleasant. Except

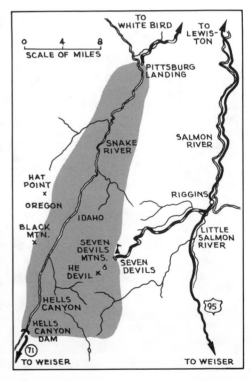

during heavy rains the road to Pittsburg Landing generally can be negotiated by an ordinary car from May 1 to the end of October.

Rafting

Folks wishing to raft, starting at Hells Canyon Dam, must obtain permits from the Forest Service many months in advance. The land is wild, the water would be a mob scene if not controlled.

Rafting in Hells Canyon

RIVER OF NO RETURN WILDERNESS

Administered by Nez Perce, Bitterroot, Payette,
Salmon, Challis, and Boise National Forests
Best season—July through September
Hiking—good
Climbing—none
Trail maps—River of No Return Wilderness,
Middle Fork Salmon (an excellent strip map of
the run), Salmon (also an excellent strip map)
Guidebook—none

In 1980 Congress put remnants of two long-established primitive areas into a single wilderness of 2.2 million acres, largest in the old 48 states, and including lands among the most pristine. The heavily traveled (by boat) rivers are the central attractions and the trails are scarcely touched except during hunting season. The country consists of open sagebrush hills up to 6500-7000 feet and above that of dry ridges covered by pine and fir forests. A few treeless peaks rise as high as 10,000 feet, with alpine lakes in cirques scooped from granite, metamorphic, and volcanic rocks. Generally the most complete solitude is found where the scenery is subtle rather than dramatic.

For 79 miles upstream from its confluence with the Snake, the Salmon is the legendary "River of No Return," running through the Salmon River Gorge, second-deepest in the nation, surpassed only by Hells Canyon. The "Breaks" on the north side are named for the narrow strip where hills break away into depths of the gorge. The famous white-water float trips have been cheapened by a parade of powerboats and within the "wilderness" there are tourist-and-hunter-serving airstrips on homesteads and a corridor road to Whitewater Ranch. Though still beautiful, the gorge no longer is truly primitive.

The 100-mile Middle Fork Salmon, a National Wild River and the only navigable stream of such length in the Northwest where powerboats are banned, is the climax of the region, marred only by airstrips on private inholdings. The most popular trip in the area is not a hike at all, but putting a raft or kayak in the water at Boundary Creek and coasting down to the Salmon River, on the way passing a number of prehistoric Indian campsites and paintings.

Access to the Salmon River Breaks is by river boat or by paved road from Dixie and then 34 miles of rough forest road either to Mackay Bar or Whitewater Ranch. Country of the former Idaho Primitive Area is very difficult to reach. Access to the west is by long trails from Mackay Bar and to the east by road from Challis to Sleeping Deer Lookout. The 30-mile tortuous track climbing to over 9000 feet is so narrow that if two cars meet often one must back up ¼ mile to a turnout.

Hiking

A trail follows the Salmon River, going constantly up and down to get over or under bluffs. Carry water and watch for rattlesnakes.

The former Idaho Primitive Area contains hundreds of miles of trails, mostly very private, there being no grand views or exciting flower fields. The east and west sides have some pleasant lakes and peaks.

Climbing

The scattering of cliffs, as in the Big Horn Crags, so far have not interested climbers.

Hiking Season

Trails are snowfree sooner, but the long and poor access roads usually are not passable until early July and are snow-closed again in late September. Summer weather is generally fair with a few thunderstorms.

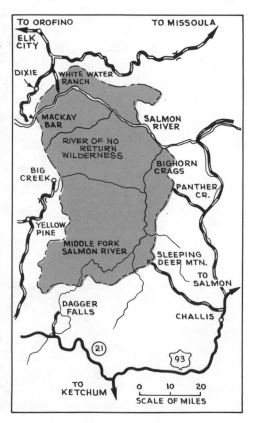

Salmon River

SELWAY-BITTERROOT WILDERNESS

Administered by Nez Perce, Clearwater, Bitterroot, and Lolo National Forests
Best season—July through September
Hiking—good
Climbing—some
Trail map—Selway-Bitterroot Wilderness
Guidebook—none

A huge wilderness by contemporary American (if not Idaho) standards, some 50 by 65 miles, the steep east side sliced by bare-cliff canyons, the western portion a vast expanse of forested ridges, with small pines predominant. Elevations range from a sagebrush-dry 2000 feet to 10,131-foot Trapper Peak. Except for a scattering of ice-sharpened granite summits and a handful of cirque lakes, little of the country is alpine in character. The lakes draw heavy traffic, as does the whole area during hunting season, but in summer, a hiker has no problem finding places to be lonesome.

The crest of the Bitterroot Mountains (named for Montana's lovely state flower, extremely rare in the mountains themselves) is the boundary between Idaho and Montana—because a government surveyor mistook the crest for the Continental Divide, the intended boundary.

The peace is not without irritants: a 10-mile thumb of logging and roads pushed deep into what should be wilderness on the east, giving cheaply-quick entry to highlands; and an airstrip at the Moose Creek Ranger Station within the wilderness on the west, maintained for public use by the Forest Service and used by commercial packers to fly in their customers, saving 25 trail miles.

Access to the west side of the wilderness is by a long, rough forest road from Elk City, to the north side from US 12 over Lolo Pass, and to the east side from US 93 in Montana.

Hiking

Trails from the west require three-four days to reach the high country so most hiking is from the east.

Trapper Peak. The highest summit in the range offers endless views of forests, interrupted only by rocky peaks to the north and farms in the Bitterroot Valley to the east. Drive 15½ miles from Darby on US 93 and Highway 473, then 6½ miles up Lavene Creek to the road-end. The trail starts in timber, ascends a ridge to views, and in 5½ miles, gaining 4000 feet, reaches the top.

Coquina Lake. Easy mountains to wander up, meadows and lakes, and miles of beargrass growing in open subalpine forest of fir, hemlock, and spruce. From US 93 north of Darby drive the Lost Horse Creek road 20 miles to Bear Creek Pass. The trail, poorly marked, seldom maintained, boggy areas churned by horses, starts here at 6100 feet and climbs in about 4 miles to the 6900-foot lake. The path passes an earth dam on Bear Creek that from the size of trees growing on it must have been built more than 50 years ago—what for and by whom the rangers don't know.

The skilled navigator equipped with topog maps can make cross-country trips south from Bear Creek Pass toward Elk Lake, alternating from Idaho to Montana as terrain dictates.

Climbing

Though most peaks are walk-ups the range is mainly solid granite and some north and east faces offer excellent rock climbing, notably the north face of Trapper Peak and the north and east faces of 9965-foot El Capitan.

Hiking Season

As Lewis and Clark found to their chagrin, snow remains on high trails until early July. Winter ordinarily doesn't return in earnest before November, but a foot or two of white sometimes is dumped on the country in September. Weather from July through September is mostly sunny; August is hot. Lightning storms are fairly common.

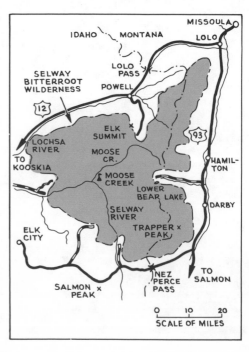

Trapper Peak

Idaho/8

SALMO-PRIEST AND SCOTCHMAN PEAK

*Administered by Colville and Idaho Panhandle
  National Forests*
Best season—mid-June through October
Hiking—good
Climbing—none
*Trail maps—Idaho Panhandle National Forest,
  Priest Lake Ranger District*
Guidebook—none

Valleys in the Salmo-Priest area are so lush they make a hiker think he is in the maritime Cascades, with hemlocks and ferns and devil's club and western red cedars up to 12 feet in diameter. Plus open subalpine forests and flower gardens on rocky little peaks. Plus a wealth of wildlife, including the only herd of mountain caribou—an endangered species—remaining in the lower 48 states.

Straddling the border of Washington and Idaho next to Canada, this southernmost extension of the Selkirk Mountains was slated for roading and logging. When local conservationists submitted petitions signed by 10,000 people asking the area be dedicated as wilderness, the Forest Service took another look and found the commercial value of the timber to be less than the cost of building logging roads. A study was made, resulting in a wilderness proposal, to which were added three others: Scotchman Peak, Mallard-Larkins, and Selkirks.

Access to the Washington side is from Highway 31 near Metaline Falls and to the Idaho side from US 2/95 near Bonners Ferry.

Hiking

Little Snowy Top offers the most representative introduction to delights of this small wildland. From US 2/95 drive the Upper Priest River road to the end. The trail follows the river about 4 miles through splendid forest, crosses the stream (find a fallen log—fording is difficult in early summer), and switchbacks 3800 feet in about 6 miles to the 6829-foot summit, the fire-lookout cabin, and vistas west over Salmo River valley and north to big peaks in Canada. Close by is 7548-foot Snowy Top, highest peak in the area.

For those seeking views and willing to forego deep forests, the Salmo Mountain road climbs to the 6828-foot lookout. From a spur road near the top find the Shedroof Mountain trail, which with many ups and downs follows the ridge 4 miles to Shedroof and 6 miles more to Little Snowy.

The Scotchman Peak area on the Idaho-Montana border has a number of steep trails to rugged peaks, most reached from the town of Clarks Fork on forest road No. 419.

Climbing—None

Hiking Season

Valley trails ordinarily are snowfree in April or May, the high country by late June. Winter snows begin in October. Sunshine generally becomes more common than rain in June, and from July through September skies are mainly clear but with intervals of grayness and occasional thunderstorms.

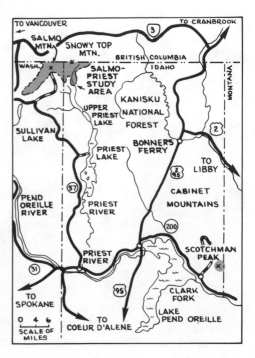

74

Savage Mountain from East Fork Peak trail

Northern California

(Above) Elk at Gold Bluff Beach, Prairie Creek Redwoods State Park
(Opposite) Redwood trees in Redwood National Park

The crater of 6907-foot Cinder Cone, Lassen Volcanic National Park

NORTHERN CALIFORNIA

1. Redwood National Park
2. Yolla Bolly-Middle Eel Wilderness
3. Trinity Alps Primitive Area
4. Marble Mountain Wilderness
5. Mt. Shasta
6. Lassen Volcanic National Park
7. Caribou and Thousand Lakes Wildernesses
8. Lava Beds National Monument
9. South Warner Wilderness

have difficulty gaining sustenance from thin air of the High Sierra.

Climbers find not much solid rock of interest, but the lofty mass of Shasta offers stimulating challenges in winter and, on the glacier routes, good sport in any season.

The question might well be asked, why would any California hiker, with all the magnificence of the Sierra Nevada to roam, ever bother to visit the northern section of the state?

The answer lies partly in the somewhat better (so far) chance to be alone, population centers far away and most of the wildlands little-famed. However, the intrinsic beauties are their own reward. Popularity of redwood groves and ocean beaches needs no explanation, nor that of the great volcanoes. But there are also mild-mannered ridgelands to the west and sky-open desert ranges to the east, stark lava beds, and in the Trinity Alps, peaks and valleys reminiscent of the North Cascades of Washington.

As elsewhere in California, summer weather is benign; the lower elevations appeal to hikers who

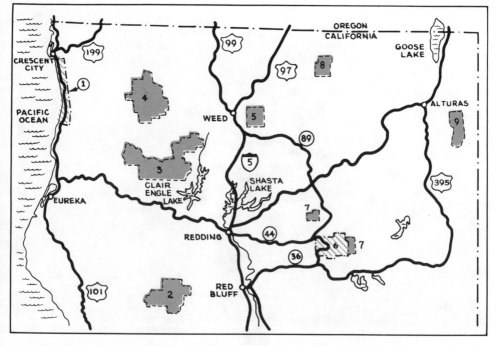

Bumpass Hell, Lassen Volcanic National Park

REDWOOD NATIONAL PARK

*Administered by Redwood National Park and
  California State Parks*
Camping permit required
Best season—year around
Hiking—excellent, though limited
Climbing—none
Trail map—Redwood National Park
Guidebook—none

Cathedral groves of coast redwoods, the tallest
trees on earth, many 500 to 1000 years old, meet
ocean beaches pounded by surf, busy with birds.
The groves were saved from lumber mills by
thousands of individuals who grouped together to
buy them for donation to state and national parks.
To fully appreciate these efforts, see the clearcuts
on private land, a shocking contrast to park forests.
Of course, industry replants clearcuts and expects
to "harvest" the next "crop" of sawlogs in less
than a century—but many, many centuries are
needed to grow a cathedral.

Tragically, the national park is "unfinished
business," Congress having failed to take steps
essential to fulfill the intent of the establishing
legislation of 1968 and protect park trees and
streams from effects of logging on private lands.

The preserved (?) redwoods are in a combination of national and state parks extending 35 miles
along the coast highway, US 101, between Cres-
cent City and Orick.

Hiking

Many short trails of ½ to 5 miles sample
forest and beach. Heavy underbrush makes
cross-country travel impractical.

The lone backpacker's trail in Redwood Park,
8½ miles long, leads to the world's tallest known
tree, 367 feet. The way parallels and twice crosses
Redwood Creek, which in summer meanders
through a wide gravel wash, spanned by temporary
footbridges. From late autumn to spring, when
most of the annual precipitation of 100 inches
falls, the creek fills the wash from bank to bank
and the bridges have to be removed. Since the
stream is too deep to ford, the hiking season on
this trail is from May to October. Backpackers
must get a park camping permit; camping is
allowed anywhere on the gravel bars except
¼ mile from Tall Tree Grove.

A stretch of hikable beach runs 10 miles north
from Orick toward Split Rock, partly paralleled
by road. Backpackers are permitted, though not
encouraged, to camp on the beach.

*Climbing—*None

Hiking Season

Trails are open the year around and are especially lovely between winter storms, when the
park is virtually deserted. Weather is mainly fair
from July through September, unpredictable the
rest of the year. Snow is seldom a problem.

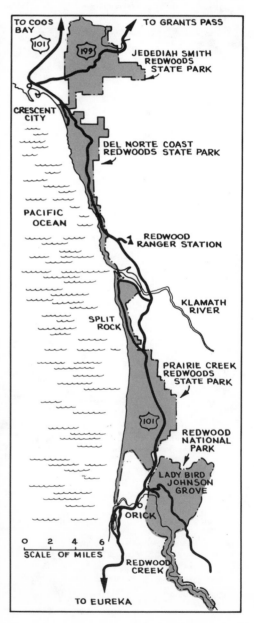

Dedication Grove

YOLLA BOLLY–MIDDLE EEL WILDERNESS

Administered by Mendocino and Shasta-Trinity National Forests
Wilderness permit required
Best season—June to mid-October
Hiking—good
Climbing—none
Trail maps—Mendocino and Shasta-Trinity National Forests (both needed)
Guidebook—none

A gentle wildland of rolling ridges and valleys. The intriguing name comes from the Indian words *yo-la* meaning "snowcovered" and *bo-li* meaning "high peak"; Middle Eel refers to the Middle Fork of the Eel River.

Solitude and peace are the specialties of the Yolla Bolly. With only a few small lakes and a relative lack of spectacular peaks, visitor use is light. All the better for quiet enjoyment of the miles and miles of forest and the scattering of ridgetop meadows. Elevations range from 2700 feet in valleys to 6000-7000-foot ridge crests to South Yolla Bolly Mountain at 8083 feet.

The wilderness is reached by driving State Highway 36 from Red Bluff.

Hiking

Because of light use trails are easy on the feet. Creeks and springs are sometimes few and far between so carry water.

Black Rock Mountain is a good sampling of the area. A 6-mile hike with a 2800-foot elevation gain leads to the 7755-foot summit and broad views north and south. To visit the center of the wilderness continue along the trail, which with ups and downs runs from one ridge to another. To find the trailhead drive a forest road 25 miles from Harrison Gulch Ranger Station.

Climbing—None

Hiking Season

Walking is pleasant from early June to mid-October. High summer can be a bit warm. Wetness is rare—from June through September the total average rainfall is less than one inch, mostly from occasional thundershowers.

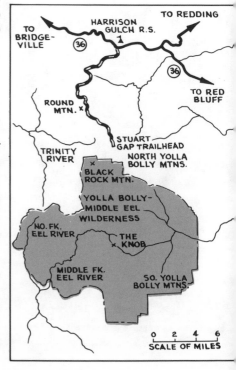

Juvenile saw-whet owls along the South Fork Cottonwood Creek trail

View south from Black Rock Mountain trail

TRINITY ALPS PRIMITIVE AREA

Administered by Shasta-Trinity and Klamath
  National Forests
Wilderness permit required
Best season – mid-June to late October
Hiking – excellent
Climbing – some
Trail map – Shasta-Trinity National Forest
Guidebook – 41 Hiking Trails of Northwest
  California

Forests and rivers, meadows and lakes, ice-carved basins and cliffs, even two living glaciers—altogether the Trinity Alps Primitive Area is a land of wild alpine enchantment, and at a low elevation for California, the highest peak 9002 feet.

Conservationists and Forest Service are united in their determination to achieve formal dedication of a wilderness. A major stumbling block is that half the area is a checkerboard of public lands intermingled with private lands dating from 19th century railroad land grants and mineral claims staked out under obsolete mining laws. Thus, a section of land that otherwise would be part of the wilderness has guest ranches on it and a road to them.

The Trinity Alps lie northwest of Redding and are bordered on the east by the people-swarming Trinity National Recreation Area around Clair Engle Reservoir.

Hiking

Most trips require two or three days minimum. For generations horse travel predominated, and continues to be heavy, so expect bouldery and dusty trails. Don't count on being lonely; more and more California hikers are driving several extra hours to escape Sierra mobs and now outnumber the horses.

Emerald and Sapphire Lakes. The prime recommendation of local rangers is a hike up the Stuart Fork of the Trinity River, 16 miles each way, elevation gain 3000 feet. The trail passes views of the Sawtooth Range and wanders through large meadows covered with flowers in late June and July.

Caribou Lakes. The most popular hike, 8½ miles each way, 2500-foot elevation gain. Reach the trail by driving the Coffee Creek road to the trailhead at Big Flat.

Climbing

All peaks can be scrambled up but there are interesting routes on granite pinnacles of the Sawtooth Range. Castle Crags State Park, near Mt. Shasta, provides other short problems.

Hiking Season

Many trails are open except for modest snow-patches in mid-June and not snowbound until late October at the earliest. June often has thunderstorms but July, August, and September generally are dry and blue-sky months.

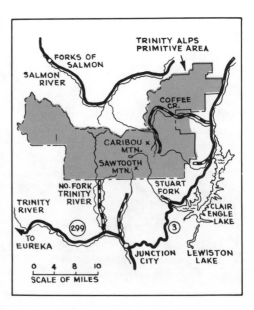

Sawtooth Ridge from the Salmon River valley

MARBLE MOUNTAIN WILDERNESS

Administered by Klamath National Forest
Wilderness permit required
Best season—mid-June to mid-October
Hiking—excellent
Climbing—none
Trail map—Klamath National Forest
*Guidebook—*Marble Mountain Wilderness, 41
  Hiking Trails of Northwest California

Deep, rocky valleys and wooded hills dotted with a few meadows and lakes, the area is named for Marble Mountain, a long ridge capped by a 1000-foot-thick layer of marble. Most trails are on 6000-7000-foot crests (the highest point is 8299-foot Boulder Peak) in relatively open country considerably cooler than the valleys, where temperatures often rise to 100°.

The wilderness, located near the northern border of California, is reached by driving west from Interstate 5 on State Highway 96.

Hiking

A good many hikers and a few horsemen visit the wilderness, mostly congregating at alpine lakes, particularly those near trails. Privacy can be found at some of the smaller, off-trail lakes; however, river bottoms are a tangle of brush and boulders and hillsides are steep and covered with thickets, so off-trail travel is not really recommended.

The Haypress trail in the south, reached by forest road from the town of Somes Bar, climbs high enough for views of the entire region. Sky High Lakes in the north, reached from Lovers Camp, are popular and beautiful Cliff Lake, reached from the Shackleford Creek road, is another favorite. The lake trails, of course, are the crowded ones; the many miles of other paths offer a chance of solitude.

Climbing

All the mountains have walk-up sides.

Hiking Season

Trails are usually snowfree from mid-June to mid-October. The annual precipitation of about 100 inches falls mainly in winter. June has spells of rain. July and August typically are fair and warm with occasional thunderstorms. September is quite variable, rain and sun alternating.

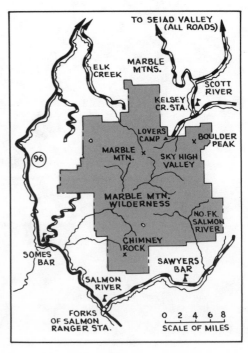

View north from Sandy Ridge trail

MT. SHASTA

Administered by Shasta-Trinity National Forest
Best season – July through October
Hiking – limited
Climbing – good
Trail map – Shasta-Trinity National Forest visitor
*   map*
Guidebook – 41 Hiking Trails of Northwest
*   California*

The huge bulk of 14,161-foot Mt. Shasta, higher by far than any other mountain within hundreds of miles and designated a National Landmark, dominates northern California. Travelers on Interstate 5 first see the cloud-lofty volcano hours before the highway finally skirts its flanks, giving near views of the double summit and half-dozen glaciers. Unfortunately, the majesty has been much abused, the wilderness effectively destroyed, partly because checkerboard ownership renders uniform management impossible.

Lower elevations are covered by impenetrable thickets of buckbrush and manzanita. Above the jungle a belt of lovely, open, and much-logged forest extends to timberline at about 8000 feet.

Hiking

Three trails are most popular.

Black Butte, 2½ miles each way. An 1800-foot elevation gain to a dramatic 360-degree viewpoint atop a 6325-foot cinder cone.

Gray Butte, an 8119-foot ridge crest reached on a 2-mile trail, mostly in forest but with openings that in June and July offer blossoms by the acre. Approximately 700 feet elevation gain.

Sierra (Club) Lodge, a 1½-mile hike through woods, ascending about 1000 feet to a stone cabin at timberline and, in season, the beginning of flowers that continue upward in delightful meadows. The cabin is open to all comers (no charge) but has only six bunks and is meant for winter ski-touring and emergencies. Camping space outside and a cool spring. Part of the trail goes through a selective logging area where the Forest Service has selected out all the shade trees. In olden days when the mountain wilderness was large the cabin played an important role as the first-night stopover for climbers who hoisted packs way down in the valley.

Climbing

About 1000 people a year attain the summit of Shasta, mainly via the "easy" south side. In May and June a pleasant all-snow walk can be made to the top; ice ax and crampons are essential since the final slopes are a bit steep. August, when little snow remains, is the most popular month; crampons rarely are needed but ice ax is recommended. The climb can start either at the Ski Bowl or from the Sierra Lodge.

The north side offers challenging routes up the Whitney, Bolam, and Hotlum Glaciers, all steep near the top and in the case of the Hotlum requiring a move off the ice to rock on the west. Ice axes, crampons, and rope are necessary.

No matter what the route, weather can be severe at 14,000 feet. Afternoon thunderstorms are common in summer. Climbers are asked to register at the Mount Shasta Sheriff's Office.

Hiking Season

The Black Butte hike is good from June through October. Snow doesn't melt from the other two trails until early July. Weather is usually fair from July through September except for afternoon thunder.

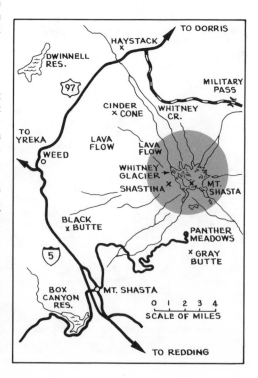

Northwest side of Mt. Shasta

LASSEN VOLCANIC NATIONAL PARK

Administered by Lassen Volcanic National Park
Camping permit required
Best season—June through October
Hiking—good
Climbing—none
Trail map—the handout map of the park is inadequate for hikers
Guidebooks—**Lassen Volcanic National Park, park trail leaflets**

Certain neglected volcanoes of the Cascades might learn a lesson from Lassen, which earned national park status by erupting some 150 times between 1914 and 1921, the great blast of 1915 being the most recent major eruption in the old 48 states—until 1980, that is, when St. Helens blew. The 150 miles of park trails lead to the summit of the 10,457-foot peak, to lava fields, cinder cones, and hot springs, and through lovely forests and alpine meadows to lakes.

The Lassen Park road crosses the park, rounding three sides of the peak and ascending to 8500 feet. Timberline is about 8000 feet, though scrub trees extend as high as 9500.

Hiking

Trails are well-marked but some cross patches of lava or cinders so the going isn't always easy. Camping permits are required for overnight hikes.

Paradise Meadow is especially famous for flower fields. The trail starts from the Lassen Park road.

Bumpass Hell, an area of fumaroles, boiling mudpots, and steaming pools, is reached by a 1½-mile trail beginning at 8200 feet near Park Road Pass. The path gains 400 feet and loses 300.

Summit of Lassen Peak. From 8500-foot Park Road Pass the trail climbs very steeply to the top, gaining 2000 feet in 2½ miles. Lava in the crater appears to have only just cooled. There is a dramatic look from the rim down the devastated area of the 1915 eruption, views south to the Sierra Nevada and Sacramento Valley and north to Mt. Shasta.

Painted Dunes, the rangers' favorite hike. The trail leaves Butte Lake in the northeast corner of the park and in 1½ miles ascends 6907-foot Cinder Cone, which was reported by pioneers to be still steaming in 1851. Wonderful view of the Fantastic Lava Beds (a recent flow, actually not so fan-

tastic), the Painted Dunes (small hills of red and yellow rock), Lassen Peak, forests and lakes. Nobel's Emigrant Wagon Trail passed the foot of the Cinder Cone and tracks remain in cinder fields.

Climbing

The few crags are so terribly rotten the climbing is extremely dangerous, not worth considering.

Hiking Season

Forest paths open in June. Such high trails as those to Bumpass Hell and the summit of Lassen usually are snowcovered until mid-July. Flowers are at their best in late July and early August. Snow generally doesn't stop hikers until November. Summer weather is mostly fair except for brief intervals of lightning.

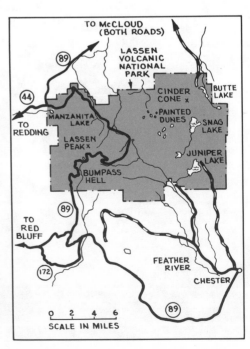

Mt. Lassen from Reflection Lake

CARIBOU AND THOUSAND LAKES WILDERNESSES

Administered by Lassen National Forest
Wilderness permit required
Best season—July through September
Hiking—good
Climbing—none
Trail map—for both areas, the Lassen National Forest map of Almanor, Eagle Lake, and Mineral Districts
Guidebook—none

Two tiny wilderness areas (the Caribou 4 miles by 7, the Thousand Lakes 5 miles by 6) in old lava flows, the country composed of 6000-7000-foot forested plateaus sprinkled with mountain lakes.

Caribou Wilderness, named for 7784-foot North and 7757-foot South Caribou Peaks, adjoins Lassen Volcanic National Park on the east. Easy access from State Highway A21 makes the trails crowded.

Thousand Lakes Wilderness, named for countless potholes in the lava but having only a dozen true lakes, is 6 miles northwest of the park. Extremely difficult road access keeps out the throngs.

Hiking

Caribou Wilderness. Forest roads from Highway A21 lead to three trailheads. The north and south entries are poorly marked and very hard to find and thus the Silver Lake-Caribou Lake entrance is the most practical. In any event no point in the wilderness lies beyond a day's round-trip walk. The extensive system of good trails is excellent for families and novices.

From the road-end at Caribou Lake a trail enters the wilderness and soon branches, the left fork leading to North Divide Lake and the right to Black Lake. The two eventually join, offering a fine overnight loop hike.

Thousand Lakes Wilderness. The most common entry is on the east side from US 89 near the town of Old Station. The forest recreation road, unmarked, crosses a magnificent logging road (where the road appropriations are spent). The last 2 miles are murder for a passenger car and may best be walked. The trail from the road-end leads in 4 miles, 800 feet elevation gain, to Lake Eiler, largest in the wilderness.

Bunchgrass and Magee Peak roads on the south side are better, but trails from them are very rough. Magee Peak is a stiff climb of 4000 feet in 5 miles to the site of a former lookout.

Climbing

No real mountains, just forested hills.

Hiking Season

Trails are generally snowfree from mid-June through October. Lakes do not thaw until later, so early July through September is the most popular season.

June through August are usually fair with only an occasional thunderstorm. Because of the elevation, days normally are mild, nights chilly. September and October typically are clear and cold.

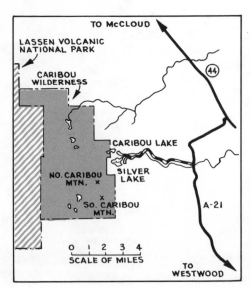

Jewel Lake, on the Black Lake trail, Caribou Wilderness

LAVA BEDS NATIONAL
MONUMENT

Administered by Lava Beds National Monument
Best season—April through November
Hiking—difficult
Climbing—none
Trail map—Lava Beds National Monument
Guidebook—none

Lava Beds is a high desert forbidding to the average backpacker but fascinating to students of vulcanism and wildlife. A small portion of the monument is proposed for wilderness status.

One can easily spend several days exploring the recent lava flows, numerous lava caves, and battlefields of the Modoc War, in which Captain Jack and a handful of Modoc Indians fought federal troops to a standstill. Most of the notable features are reached by short nature trails (under 1 mile).

Deer are best seen in winter, antelope in summer, and waterfowl in spring and fall. The best (which is very little) chance to spot bobcats is in summer when their food supply—small animals—is abundant.

The monument borders the Tule Lake Wildlife Refuge, famous for waterfowl.

Hiking

The ambitious hiker wanting to get away from nature walks must strike off cross-country through rough terrain of no water and many rattlesnakes.

If experienced and really determined, he can visit the Black Lava Flow, among the newest in the Northwest. Roaming the desert in the north of the monument, he is likely to see not only deer, antelope, and snakes but perhaps bobcats and bighorn sheep.

Climbing—None

Hiking Season

Due to a 4000-foot elevation, summer temperatures seldom rise above 85°. Clouds occasionally float overhead but the meager annual precipitation of 12 inches mainly comes as winter snows. Though hikable the year around, the area gets pretty cold in winter.

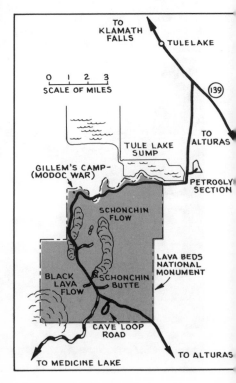

Deer near Skull Cave

Skull Cave

SOUTH WARNER WILDERNESS

Administered by Modoc National Forest
Wilderness permit required
Best season – July through September
Hiking – excellent
Climbing – none
Trail map – Modoc National Forest
Guidebook – none

The Warner Mountains, an isolated spur of the Cascades, are high, open country, far enough inland to have a dry, cold climate. West slopes are gently rounded but on east exposures glaciers have scooped cliffs dropping to delightful basins. Access roads climb to 6500 feet and the Summit trail traverses a 9000-foot alpine ridge for nearly 15 miles.

From the crest of the narrow range one looks over mountains and plains of three states, and also east and west down to ranches from which cattle annually ascend to summer in the highlands. Presently the wilderness is little used for recreation, and mainly in the vicinity of the two alpine lakes; when more people arrive perhaps the cattle will depart.

Timberline is about 8000 feet. Above are vast meadows of sagebrush and lupine interspersed with groves of twisted pine.

Forest road access on the west is from Alturas and on the east from Cedarville.

Hiking

Hikers are more numerous every year and currently are roughly equal in numbers to horsemen. Hunting season is still dominated by horses.

Patterson Lake on the Summit trail is perhaps the prettiest hike in the wilderness, and certainly is the most popular. Trails lead in from either side, the 6-mile west approach having the advantage of going through Pine Creek Basin and the 8-mile east approach of climbing past gaudy cliffs.

Pine Creek Basin potentially is one of the beauty spots of northern California, with a meandering creek, lush greenery, and meadows rolling upward to high ridges. However, the scene long was a fright, several hundred cows beating the soil to death and dirtying streams beyond use. Sympathy for the ranchers who pioneered the area diminishes when damage to the ecosystem is viewed. Happily, the situation is improving gradually. Some cows

linger but clean campsites and drinkable (with treatment?) water can be found.

Climbing – None

Hiking Season

Trails are generally open from the beginning of July until snow falls in mid-October. July and August are fair except for a few thunderstorms. September has a little bad weather and the nights are very cold.

Pine Creek Basin

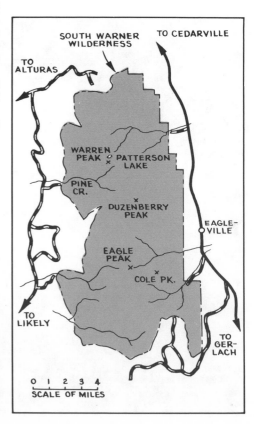

Oregon

(Above) Glacier Lake, Eagle Cap Wilderness
(Below) Crater Lake National Park

Beargrass and Mt. Hood

OREGON

1. Kalmiopsis and Wild Rogue Wildernesses
2. Mountain Lakes Wilderness–Sky Lakes—proposed wilderness
3. Crater Lake National Park
4. Diamond Peak Wilderness
5. Three Sisters Wilderness
6. Mt. Washington Wilderness
7. Mt. Jefferson Wilderness
8. Mt. Hood Wilderness and Columbia Gorge
9. Gearhart Mountain Wilderness
10. Steens Mountain and Hart Mountain Antelope Range
11. Strawberry Mountain Wilderness
12. Eagle Cap Wilderness

Other Wilderness Study Areas
A. Cummins Creek

The Oregon Cascades are volcanic in origin, the climbing either on glaciers or rotten rock. Few valley forests remain intact and most hiking therefore is in subalpine forests, parkland, and meadows. The Wallowa Mountains, though of much sounder rock and containing the largest single alpine area in the state, are great for hiking but offer little climbing. Other ranges are entirely walking terrain.

The number of wilderness areas is impressive but they are mainly tiny preserves and the total acreage protected is woefully inadequate. The tragic flaw of the mountains is to lie in the world's best region for growing coniferous forests and to be very easy to log. Oregon leads the nation in timber production and the U.S. Forest Service has no intention of sparing any trees worth cutting. However, conservationists are gathering strength and have put forward proposals for the full length of the Cascades and for other mountain areas to save as much as possible of the as-yet-unruined country.

Mt. Jefferson from Park Ridge,
Mt. Jefferson Wilderness

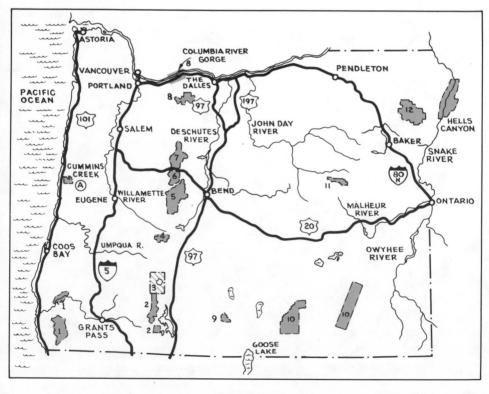

KALMIOPSIS AND WILD ROGUE WILDERNESSES

Administered by Siskiyou National Forest
Wilderness permit required
Best season—Kalmiopsis, mid-May to mid-October; Wild Rogue, spring and fall
Hiking—fair
Climbing—none
Trail map—Kalmiopsis and Wild Rogue Wildernesses, Wild and Scenic Rogue River
Guidebook—Guide to Kalmiopsis Wilderness

The Kalmiopsis Wilderness, in the Siskiyou Mountains within view of the ocean, was set aside for its unique botanical interest, the flora including two pre-Ice Age relics, the extremely rare *kalmiopsis leachiana*, a member of the heath family resembling a miniature rhododendron, and Brewer or weeping spruce. Though lacking spectacular vistas the country offers solitude.

Reminders of the mining era are present everywhere. Artifacts may be found from the gold rush of the 1850s—and pits and truck roads of the World War II chrome mines.

Access to the wilderness on the east side is from US 199 near Grants Pass, but the last few miles of approach roads are four-wheel-drive and thus the best access is on the west side from US 101 near Brookings. Take the road signed Loeb State Park and drive about 35 miles to the wilderness boundary.

Though the Wild Rogue Wilderness is most famed for float trips down the 84 miles of river classified as Wild, Scenic, or Recreational, the trail offers another way to experience scenery of forest and stream—and the parade of floaters.

Access to the west end of the trail is from US 101 at Gold Beach, to the east from Interstate 5 or US 199 near Grants Pass.

Hiking

Kalmiopsis. Easy trails lead to 4600-foot Vulcan Peak (only 1½ miles) and tiny Vulcan Lake. The Dry Butte trail passes through a large patch of *kalmiopsis leachiana*, which blooms in late May or early June. The Heather Mountain trail on the north side is dry, so carry water.

The classic hike is the Upper Chetco trail, signed Boulder Creek Trail, beginning near Long Ridge Lookout. The route leads across the wilderness, several times dropping to the unbelievably clear waters of the Chetco River.

Northwest of the wilderness is the Big Craggies Botanical Area, a virgin site set aside for scientific studies.

Wild Rogue Wilderness. The Rogue River trail runs 40 miles along the north bank from Grave Creek to Foster Bar, a splendid five-day ramble. For shorter hikes a road to Marial gives access to the middle section.

Climbing—None

Hiking Season

Snow melts from Kalmiopsis trails in mid-May, or sometimes late April, and doesn't return until late October or November. May weather varies from perfect to daily rain, June and July have occasional showers, August is hot and dry, and September and October are again variable.

Due to the low elevation, Rogue hiking is mighty warm in summer; spring and fall are much pleasanter.

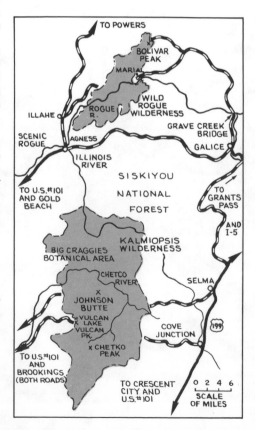

Rafting on the Rogue River

MOUNTAIN LAKES WILDERNESS – SKY LAKES

Administered by Winema and Rogue River National Forests
Wilderness permit required in Mountain Lakes
Best season – July through September
Hiking – excellent
Climbing – none
Trail maps – Sky Lakes User's Guide, Mountain Lakes Wilderness
Guidebook – Pacific Crest Trail, Volume 2

The tiny (6 square miles) Mountain Lakes Wilderness contains a score of tree-surrounded lakes, all very small except Lake Harriet, several peaks poking heads above timberline, a scattering of little meadows, and flowers growing in nooks and crannies of rock outcrops. The country is high, from 5000 feet to 8208-foot Aspen Butte, and getting to the better lakes is hard enough to keep the population at a reasonable level.

The much larger and more popular Sky Lakes area, a 5-mile-wide corridor extending 23 miles south along the Pacific Crest Trail from Crater Lake National Park, is being studied for classification as wilderness and meanwhile is administered as such except for allowing snowmobiles south of Wickiup Trail in winter. Elevations range from 5500 feet to 7582-foot Devils Peak. The land is heavily forested with fir, spruce, hemlock, and pine, broken by innumerable lakes and a number of small meadows. Trees thin out somewhat in the north end, which is quite dry — there is no dependable drinking water from Crater Lake Park 10 miles south to Ranger Springs, where water bubbles from an arid mountainside into a deep, cool, clear pool. Views are scarce on forest trails, though the volcanic cone of 9495-foot Mt. McLoughlin lies between the Mountain Lakes and the Sky Lakes.

The Mountain Lakes Wilderness is best reached from Lake of the Woods on Highway 140. The Sky Lakes have numerous approaches, the most-used being from Four Mile Lake, also reached from Highway 140.

Hiking

The larger lakes in both areas are crowded; look elsewhere for camping.

Trails are excellent, if a bit too horse-pounded. A loop trail links most of the Mountain Lakes. The Pacific Crest Trail passes many of the Sky Lakes;

Seven Lakes Basin, the easiest access from Highway 62 at Fort Klamath, offers a dramatic view of Devils Peak, whose summit panorama includes Mt. McLoughlin and Mt. Shasta to the south and Klamath Lake east.

A trail climbs 4000 feet in 6 miles to the summit of Mt. McLoughlin, a former lookout site.

Climbing – None

Hiking Season

Snow generally melts from trails in early July and stays away until mid-October. July and August are mostly fair, with occasional thunderstorms and sometimes a week of bad weather right in the middle of summer. September is about the same only cooler. October is tricky.

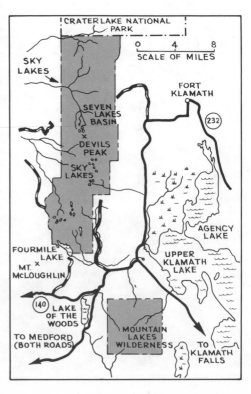

Mt. McLoughlin from the Mountain Lakes loop trail

CRATER LAKE NATIONAL PARK

Administered by Crater Lake National Park and
Umpqua National Forest
Park Service camping permit required for Pacific
Crest Trail
Best season—mid-July through mid-October
Hiking—limited
Climbing—none
Trail maps—Park Service mini-map and Umpqua
National Forest Recreation Map (both inade-
quate for hikers)
Guidebook—Pacific Crest Trail, Volume 2

The volcano known as Mt. Mazama probably was the highest peak in Oregon until 6600 years ago. Then a series of cataclysmic explosions vividly recalled in Indian legends blew clouds of ash high in the sky, winds carrying pumice throughout the Northwest and all the way to Alberta. In the aftermath the mountain collapsed into the emptied lava chamber, and after a period of burping up small cinder cones, became quiet. Only remnants of Mazama are left and it is better known for the water that filled the caldera, Crater Lake.

Conservationists are proposing new wilderness areas for the Crater Lake region: the Sky Lakes to the south; to the north, a wildland corridor along the Pacific Crest Trail to Mt. Thielsen and the Diamond Peak Wilderness.

Paved highways lead to the park from US 97 on the east and Medford on the west.

Hiking

Construction of the caldera-rim road destroyed any chance for significant pedestrianism in the park but several short paths are rewarding. A 1-mile trail ascends Wizard Island, a cinder cone rising from the lake; the island is reached by tour boat. A 1¾-mile trail climbs 1000 feet to the 8060-foot summit of Garfield Peak, with spectacular views of the lake. A 2-mile trail to the top of 8926-foot Mt. Scott, highest peak in the park, gives distant views of the lake and a broad panorama of the Klamath Lake valley and the Cascade Range south to Mt. Shasta.

The Pacific Crest Trail passes through the west side of the park, providing lonesomeness but little else of great interest. The Diamond Lake vicinity outside the park has better hiking.

Mt. Bailey is a 3000-foot climb to the 8363-foot summit, a former lookout site with magnificent views. Steep snow blocks the trail until August.

The most dramatic peak in the area is 9172-foot Mt. Thielsen, the stripped-bare plug of an old volcano. A trail starts from the trailer court at 5108-foot Diamond Lake and climbs 3 miles in timber to a junction with the Pacific Crest Trail, along which 1 mile north is a viewpoint directly under the towering red and yellow cliffs.

Climbing

The park has nothing for climbers; Thielsen, though, offers a hike and scramble up the south side.

Hiking Season

July and August and often September are generally fair with only occasional bits of bad weather. The land is high and snow doesn't completely melt from trails until mid-July; an experienced hiker could safely cross snowpatches before then but the Park Service permits no use of paths until they are worry-free for people in street shoes. Snow blocks the trails about mid-October.

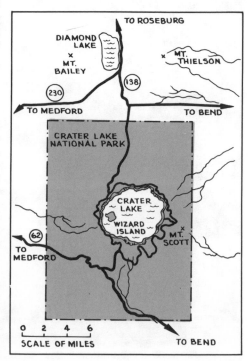

Mt. Thielsen rising above mist-covered Diamond Lake

DIAMOND PEAK WILDERNESS

Administered by Deschutes and Willamette
  National Forests
Wilderness permit required
Best season—mid-June through October
Hiking—good
Climbing—poor
Trail map—Diamond Peak Wilderness
*Guidebook—**Pacific Crest Trail, Volume 2***

This small wilderness (about 6 by 8 miles) is centered on the snow-capped roots of an old volcano, 8744-foot Diamond Peak, and the 7100-foot and 7138-foot lava crags of Mt. Yoran. The peaks are flanked by forested ridges, three tree-rimmed lakes, and a number of lakelets. The area lies amid a ring of highways and resorts, plus excellent logging roads which have put every gem of the wilderness in reach of a short walk.

To save something of what is left, conservationists are proposing new wildernesses northward through the Waldo Lake vicinity to the Three Sisters Wilderness, completing a necklace of protected wildlands along the Pacific Crest Trail from Sky Lakes to Mt. Jefferson.

Diamond Peak Wilderness is readily accessible from Highway 58, a major cross-Cascade route. One of the best views of Diamond Peak is from the highway at Odell Lake.

Hiking

The Pacific Crest Trail is magnificently scenic as it passes Diamond and Yoran on the east slopes, at timberline. As a result it is heavily traveled, as are all the lake paths. Other trails are well-maintained but not overpopulated.

The Mt. Yoran trail, starting from the Hemlock Butte road, doesn't climb the mountain but leads to a knoll offering good views both of Yoran and Diamond; since it touches no lakes, the path provides solitude.

Climbing

The snowfields and rock-jumbles of Diamond Peak require no special equipment, though an ice ax is handy. The usual route is on the south but any side will do. Mt. Yoran takes some tough scrambling and possibly a rope.

Hiking Season

Trails are passable by mid-June, though snow may linger another month around Notch Lake. The winter white comes in late October or so. As is true generally of the Oregon Cascades, summer weather is mostly fair, but once or several times blue skies are lost for days in drizzle and cloud.

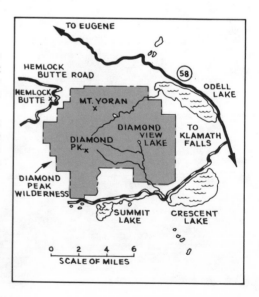

Mt. Yoran

THREE SISTERS WILDERNESS

Administered by Deschutes and Willamette National Forests
Wilderness permit required
Best season—May through November
Hiking—excellent but crowded
Climbing—fair
Trail maps—Three Sisters Wilderness and Willamette National Forest
Guidebooks—Pacific Crest Trail, Volume 2; 62 Hiking Trails, Central Oregon Cascades

Faith, Hope, and Charity they were called by pioneer settlers, and The Shining Mountains by the late Dave Simons in proposing they become, with Mt. Jefferson, the heart of an Oregon Volcanoes National Park. The richest display of vulcanism in the whole Cascade Range is here: the 10,000-foot volcanoes of the Three Sisters; the colorful core of an older volcano, 9173-foot Broken Top; the smooth slopes of a young volcano, 9050-foot Mt. Bachelor; a profusion of cinder cones; enormous and rough and very recent lava flows, some with lava tubes, others glittering with glassy obsidian; pumice fields. And there is much more in this largest and most popular of Oregon Cascades wilderness areas—hundreds upon hundreds of lakes and ponds in subalpine forest and a few nestled high in moraines; flower-bright meadows; glaciers and meltwater streams. If this country isn't of national park caliber, as Dave Simons declared, what is?

An old fire lookout road to the wilderness boundary on the east has brought motorcycles into green meadows and soft pumice slopes of McArthur Ridge and Broken Top. Though the Forest Service has forbidden wheels the tracks will remain for generations—and enforcement is so difficult that outlaws continue the gouging.

French Pete Creek, one of only two long, low-elevation, virgin-forested valleys left in western Oregon, was added to the wilderness after years of controversy.

Access to the southern part of the wilderness is from the Cascade Lakes Highway (Oregon 46) starting at Bend on the east, to the northern part from Highway 242 over McKenzie Pass and to French Pete Creek from Highway 242 via a forest road past Cougar Reservoir.

Hiking

If solitude is wanted come in early summer when snow is deep or in late fall—the latter being not only largely people-free but totally bug-free. At the height of the season an average of 100 people a day, and 300 on weekends, visit Green Lakes at the base of South Sister. The "land of a million lakes" south of the volcanoes, centered on Mink Lake and Horse Lake, similarly is mobbed by hikers, plus troops of cavalry. Ditto for the west side of the wilderness, traversed by the Pacific Crest Trail, which has few lakes but beautiful and beloved meadows, especially around Sunshine Shelter. There are, nevertheless, islands of quiet in the wilderness (the secrets not to be revealed here).

Green Lakes deserve popularity for the many-colored lava walls of South Sister on one side, Broken Top on the other, and the wildflower gardens tucked amid the chaos of black lava flows and the broad fields of yellow pumice. The trail starts from the Cascade Lakes Highway near Sparks Lake and in 6 easy and beautiful forest miles climbs 1100 feet to the 6550-foot shores.

Campfires are not allowed within 1 mile (distance subject to change) of the Green Lakes. For more private camping, continue past Green Lakes a mile, then leave the trail and go hide in the lava.

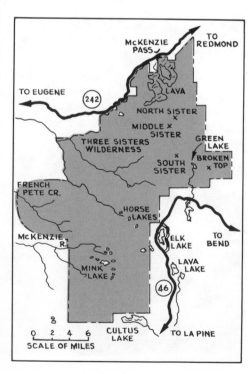

Climbing

The *North Sister*, 10,094 feet, is the most difficult, involving a hazardous traverse on crumbling lava cliffs, some steep talus, and some equally steep and perhaps very hard snow. Ice ax, crampons, and rope are needed. Access is from Frog Campground on Highway 242 with an overnight stop at Sunshine Meadows.

Middle Sister, 10,053 feet, is considerably easier but climbers are well-advised to carry ice gear. The approach is the same as for North Sister —and eager peakbaggers often do both the same day, or even all three.

South Sister, 10,354 feet, is a walk-up from Green Lakes; boots have beaten a trail of sorts to the top. The special delight of the summit crater is a little lake, the highest in Oregon, almost perpetually frozen. Views are broad and glorious up and down the length of the Cascades, west toward the Willamette Valley, and east over the High Lava Plains.

Hiking Season

French Pete Creek is usually snowfree by late May, other trails by early July. The high country closes in mid-October while French Pete normally stays open through November. July and August are mainly fair but spells of rain and drizzle must be expected, and fog on the west side.

Broken Top

MT. WASHINGTON WILDERNESS

Administered by Deschutes and Willamette National Forests
Wilderness permit required
Best season – late June through October
Hiking – limited and rough
Climbing – poor
Trail map – Mt. Washington Wilderness
Guidebooks – Pacific Crest Trail, Volume 2; 62 Hiking Trails, Central Oregon Cascades

Toss into a fairly small pot Moon-desolate lava, subalpine trees, mountain lakes, and a garnish of meadows. Stir well and serve up as the Mt. Washington Wilderness. Savor the entire dish, rough rock as well as sweet flowers.

Fully half the wilderness is covered by the McKenzie Lava Flow which boiled out near 6869-foot Belknap Crater and its satellite Little Belknap Crater. The most recent eruption perhaps came within the last 2000 years, mostly as *aa*, block lava which during final cooling split into small pieces. Numerous ridges and hollows make travel miserable; even trails are difficult, the tread composed of little, aggravating, shifting chunks. The first scientists to visit the area thought the flows were a few hundred years old—and for sure the lava looks like it solidified only yesterday, though a scattering of gnarled trees and bleached snags, themselves of great age, prove much time has passed since the hot old days.

The forests and meadows are located in the southwest and north corners of the wilderness and on a few lava-surrounded islands. What little soil there is consists of dry pumice, so vegetation is sparse.

The wilderness, which links Three Sisters Wilderness on the south and Mt. Jefferson Wilderness on the north, is easily accessible from US 20 over Santiam Pass on the north and Highway 242 over McKenzie Pass on the south.

Hiking

The Pacific Crest Trail traverses the wilderness, offering a cross-section of lava and flowers. To sample the lava on a day trip, hike the Pacific Crest Trail 3 miles north from McKenzie Pass to Little Belknap Crater, past several spatter cones and at least one walk-through conduit. Be sure to carry water, a scarce commodity hereabouts.

Climbing

The deeply glacier-eroded volcano for which the wilderness is named, 7794-foot Mt. Washington, is the only peak. Masochistic fans of crumbling lava climb the north, west and south sides. Even the easiest route requires pitons for safety—and someday a final piton will bring the entire mountain tumbling down.

Hiking Season

Trails are passable, though with snowpatches, by late June and ordinarily stay open through October. Weather is generally good in July and August except for intervals of rain and fog. September and October are unpredictable—some years beautiful, others cold and wet.

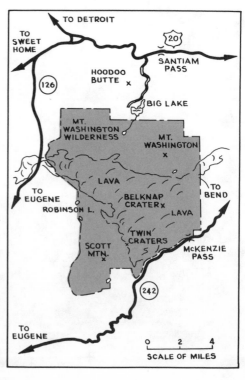

Mt. Washington from Little Belknap Crater

MT. JEFFERSON WILDERNESS

Administered by Deschutes, Mt. Hood, and Willamette National Forests
Wilderness permit required
Best season – July to mid-October
Hiking – excellent
Climbing – good
Trail map – Mt. Jefferson Wilderness
Guidebooks – 62 Hiking Trails, Central Oregon Cascades; 60 Hiking Trails, Northern Oregon Cascades

This wilderness contains a 10,437-foot glacier-draped volcano whose summit view extends north to Mt. Rainier; the 7841-foot remnant spire of an older volcano, Three Fingered Jack; cinder cones and lava flows; the largest alpine meadow in the Oregon Cascades; a sprinkling of high lakes; and some of the most popular trails in the state.

The dream of conservationists is that Mt. Jefferson, with the Three Sisters, will someday form the nucleus of an Oregon Volcanoes National Park, an inevitable companion to the national parks of Rainier, Crater Lake, and Lassen.

Mt. Jefferson rises from the Cascade Crest south of Mt. Hood. US 20-22 over Santiam Pass gives access to the south side of the wilderness and forest roads to the west and north edges. East approaches are closed to the public, lying in the Warm Springs Indian Reservation.

Hiking

Lake-dotted Jefferson Park, in some opinion the loveliest meadow in the state, spreads green lawns and flower gardens at the northern base of the volcano. The trail is reached from Detroit on Highway 22, then forest road to Breitenbush Lake. From the campground at the lake the Pacific Crest Trail climbs 1500 feet to cross 7000-foot Park Ridge and drops 1100 feet to Jefferson Park, 6 miles from the road. Use is extremely heavy; camping, if done at all, should be fireless and "no trace."

The meadows and subalpine forests of Eight Lakes Basin sprawl beneath the crags of Three Fingered Jack. Jorn Lake is considered the most scenic and certainly is the most crowded. The best plan is to see it, then go camp at a more private spot away from lakes and gardens. The trail begins at the end of the Marion Creek road, which branches from Highway 22, and in 8 miles gains about 2000 feet.

Climbing

Mt. Jefferson offers an easy if tricky walk on the south up snow and a rocky ridge; an intermediate ice climb up the Whitewater Glacier on the east; and a more difficult ascent of Jefferson Park Glacier on the north. Ice-climbing gear is needed since even on the south the snowpatches can be very steep and hard. Jefferson Park is the usual basecamp.

Three Fingered Jack supplies fans of lava cliffs a number of routes of varying difficulty, all requiring rope and hard hat.

Hiking Season

Trails are open enough for hiking in early July, though most years snowpatches linger on Park Ridge until September. Winter snows return in middle or late October. July and August generally are fair except for a few rainy spells and occasional lightning storms. Often the September clouds melt away for a beautiful and crisp Indian summer.

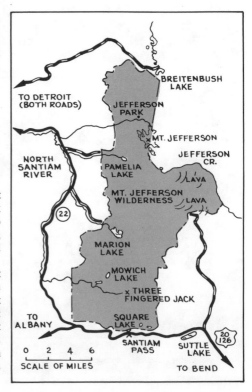

Jefferson Park and Mt. Jefferson

MT. HOOD WILDERNESS AND COLUMBIA GORGE

Administered by Mount Hood National Forest
Wilderness permit required (wilderness only)
Best season—mid-July through October up high,
*   all year in the Gorge*
Trail maps—Mt. Hood Wilderness, Mt. Hood Na-
*   tional Forest Recreation Map (inadequate for*
*   hikers), Forest Trails of the Columbia Gorge*
Guidebooks—60 Hiking Trails, Northern
*   Oregon Cascades; 35 Hiking Trails,*
*   Columbia River Gorge*

Together with Mt. St. Helens and Mt. Adams to the north, 11,235-foot Mt. Hood is one of the three Guardians of the Columbia. The lovely pyramid of the glacier-white volcano is a landmark throughout a great expanse of two states. The wilderness mainly is rock and ice. Forested ridges are being logged and meadows of the south slope are commercialized by ski lifts that climb as high as 10,000 feet. Just an hour's drive from Portland, whose skyline it dominates, the mountain is mobbed the year around.

Mt. Hood is unique for miles and miles of rhododendrons, in many places forming impenetrable thickets of bushes 10 feet tall. Blossoms begin in early June down low, the color show moving up the slopes to end at higher elevations in mid-July.

Conservationists propose wilderness protection for several nearby low-elevation valleys so far unlogged, and a wilderness to guard the Pacific Crest Trail from Hood to the Columbia River. They further are seeking better statutory protection of the Columbia Gorge, some of whose canyons and waterfalls on the precipitous Oregon side are as wild now as when Lewis and Clark came through in 1805.

The mountain is encircled by roads. US 26 traverses the south flanks and US 197 climbs high on the east side.

Hiking

The around-the-mountain Timberline trail is the classic trip, the 40-mile circuit alternating between garden ridges and forest valleys. To fully enjoy the scenery four days should be allowed and five or six are better. The route nears roads in several places, so highlights can be visited on day hikes.

To sample the Columbia Gorge, see the Forest Service map and the guidebooks.

Climbing

By conservative estimate 5000 people a year reach the summit of Hood via the south side; a few hundred annually climb the more difficult routes, such as the Eliot Glacier on the north. Though the south-side ascent takes only eight round-trip hours from Timberline Lodge, most climbers start about midnight to be off the snowfields before morning sun turns them to bogs. The glacier routes, including the Eliot, become badly crevassed by midsummer and are best done before mid-June; all are very steep, subject to avalanches, and require ice ax, rope, and crampons. The rock on ridge routes is steep and rotten; helmets are recommended.

Hiking Season

The Columbia Gorge is open the entire year, the higher trails in mid-July. Snow often closes meadow trails in mid-October. Summer weather is generally fair but week-long periods of rain and fog must be expected in July and September.

Ramona Falls on the Yocum Ridge trail

GEARHART MOUNTAIN WILDERNESS

Administered by Fremont National Forest
Best season – July through October
Hiking – fair
Climbing – none
Trail map – Gearhart Mountain Wilderness
Guidebook – none

This old volcanic dome, sculptured by Ice Age glaciers, now consists of ridges covered with lodgepole pine and whitebark pine, a number of meadows and small wet areas with a fair display of wildflowers in season, fascinating rock formations, and one mountain lake. The southern portion of the small (6 miles square) wilderness is the lowest, about 6500 feet, and supports stands of ponderosa pine mixed with firs. The higher ridges of the north, about 7000-8000 feet, are covered by lodgepole pine. All the forests are open enough to negotiate without trail and, in fact, to fully enjoy the country one should leave the beaten path and poke around in odd corners, especially in the interesting rocks and long views on ridges and the pretty little springs and meadows below.

Gearhart Mountain Wilderness, located in south central Oregon near Lakeview, is surrounded by logging roads, but the last couple miles to trailheads are on recreation roads which are mostly tortuous and sometimes best walked.

Hiking

The wilderness has only 14 miles of trail, few spectacular attractions, and except for the shores of Blue Lake few people.

The most popular entry is from the north, in 2 miles reaching Blue Lake. The second-most popular is from Lookout Rock a short mile to the Palisades, a group of weathered rocks resembling pillars and toadstools; the trail continues 8 miles to 8364-foot Gearhart Mountain and 4 miles more to Blue Lake.

One of the more picturesque meadows is in the cirque called "Head of Dairy Creek," reached by the Gearhart trail in some 5 miles from Lookout Rock. Early in July this and smaller meadows make a good showing of shooting star and buttercups, with bog orchid and elephant head in wetter spots. Near Blue Lake are some two-foot-high onion plants.

The wilderness map notes numerous springs that run all summer; however, boiling or iodine treatment may be advisable. Overnighters may find it best to leave the ridgetop trails and drop into valleys to camp by major streams.

Climbing – None

Hiking Season

Trails are usually snowfree from the end of June through October. July and August are warm and dry with occasional thunderstorms. September is pleasant, generally fair and cool, and October unsettled.

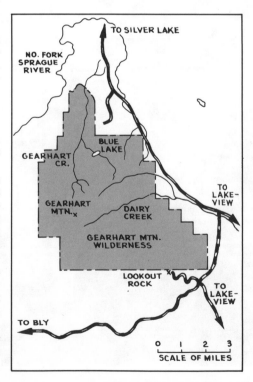

Rock formations in the Palisades Rocks area

STEENS MOUNTAIN AND HART MOUNTAIN NATIONAL ANTELOPE REFUGE

region is crawling with hunters so spring is the best time for a trip; also, the meadows are green then and water available by melting snow. Steens Mountain road, however, is usually blocked by snowbanks until mid-June.

Administered by Hart Mountain National Antelope Range and the Bureau of Land Management
Best season—May and June, September and October
Hiking—poor
Climbing—none
Trail maps—Hart Mountain National Antelope Refuge brochure, Steens Mountain (BLM)
Guidebook—none

Two fault-block mountain ranges push high above sagebrush flats, shallow lakes, and barren deserts in southeastern Oregon. Few trees break the sweep of grassy ridges. Neither is dedicated wilderness but conservationists insist both should be, before the ATV crowd demands its "right" to gouge the sagebrush and meadow communities with ruts.

The Malheur National Wildlife Refuge, below the mile-high north side of Steens Mountain, is visited in spring and fall by thousands of geese; in summer countless nesting birds feed on swarms of insects. Hart Mountain is the summer range of antelope and bighorn sheep, as well as a resting place for migratory waterfowl.

Steens Mountain is best reached from Burns; Hart Mountain, from Lakeview.

Hiking

Neither mountain has any formal provision for hikers but there is no brush in this wide-open, wide-sky country to hinder progress and except in hunting season virtually no people.

A road climbs the sloping west side of Steens Mountain from French Glen, giving access to a sketchy trail into Kiger Gorge and to meadows along the crest.

Hart Mountain is reached by a rough road from the refuge headquarters, then by walking a series of ridges to the 7710-foot summit.

In both areas be sure to carry water.

Climbing—None

Hiking Season

Weather is generally fair most of the year but July and August are hot and in fall much of the

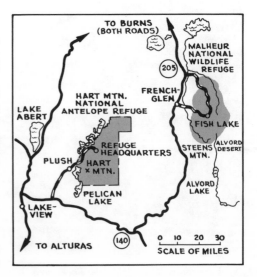

Pronghorn antelope in Hart Mountain National Antelope Range

Sandhill crane in Malheur National Wildlife Refuge

STRAWBERRY MOUNTAIN WILDERNESS

Administered by Malheur National Forest
Best season—early June to mid-October
Hiking—fair
Climbing—none
Trail map—Strawberry Mountain Wilderness
Guidebook—none

This long (18 miles), narrow (2-5 miles) wilderness straddles the backbone of the Strawberry Mountains, mostly forested but with considerable ridgetop meadowland. From the crest one looks down on either side to farms, and views also include desert basins and the Blue Mountains and far-away volcanoes of the Cascades. California bighorn sheep have been planted and chances of a sighting are good.

The Strawberry Mountains are quickly accessible from US 26 near John Day.

Hiking

The most popular hike is an easy 1½ miles to Strawberry Lake. Other trips take more sweat, including those to the summit of 9044-foot Strawberry Mountain and to Slide Lake. The full length of the wilderness is traversed by the Skyline trail, 14 miles, Pine Creek trail, 6 miles, and Canyon Mountain trail, 15 miles.

Climbing

All peaks have walk-up sides. The few cliffs are not exciting enough to draw climbers.

Hiking Season

Hiking begins in early June, though considerable snow then remains in high passes; check with the rangers at John Day or Prairie City to make sure access roads are drivable.

June is about half sunshine, half showers of rain or sometimes snow. July and August are clear except for occasional thunderstorms. Rain starts in early September but may go away for a lovely Indian summer in late September and October—which unfortunately is a time of heavy hunter traffic.

Strawberry Lake

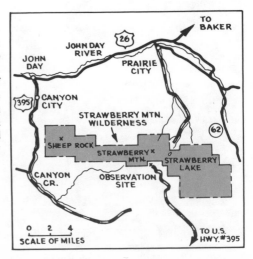

122

EAGLE CAP WILDERNESS

Administered by Wallowa-Whitman National
* Forest*
Wilderness permit required
Best season—July to mid-October
Hiking—excellent
Climbing—limited
Trail map—Eagle Cap Wilderness
Guidebook—none

Some Oregonians, not entirely enraptured by volcanoes, declare the Wallowa Mountains are the state's finest and the Eagle Cap Wilderness its grandest. The rocks are a mix of greenstone, marble, granite, and basalt uplifted by faulting. Ice Age glaciers broadened valleys, down which the rivers sparkle, and scooped the cirques which hold more than 50 lakes. Forests are varied and delightful, as are the large alpine meadows and the numerous snow-capped peaks, the highest being 9845-foot Matterhorn. (The wilderness takes its name from 9595-foot Eagle Cap.)

Located in the northeast corner of the state, the wilderness is reached on the north by paved road from Enterprise to Wallowa Lake, a popular recreation area, and on the south by forest roads branching from Highways 203 and 86.

Hiking

Horsemen constitute about 20 percent of the visitors. Unfortunately, 90 percent of all visits, equine and human, are to the mere 15 percent of the wilderness around Lake Basin; pretty as it is, the mobs, and the restrictions necessary to rehabilitate denuded lakeshores make for such aggravation the scene is best shunned.

Glacier Lake. Also very crowded. The 12-mile trail starts at 4700-foot Wallowa Lake and climbs to the shores at 8500 feet. At this and every other busy high lake, the wise plan is to camp in a valley and day-hike to the scenic splendor. At any site, popularity demands careful attention to "no trace camping," wood is scarce and a stove essential.

Ice Lake. An 8-mile trail from Wallowa Lake gains 3200 feet to the 7900-foot lake under cliffs of the Matterhorn. Fishermen stand elbow to elbow on the shores.

Bonny Lakes. The initial 6 miles of the trail are jammed, but beyond Aneroid Lake and its fish the country gets lonesome; the end of the 9½ miles to 8200-foot Bonny Lakes may be com-
pletely people-free. The peaks are less spectacular than elsewhere in the wilderness but the broad valleys nourish some of the best flower fields. A wonderful 10-mile loop can be taken from the lakes, dropping a couple miles into Sheep Creek, then following a long ridge back toward Aneroid Lake.

To enjoy quintessential Wallowa beauty—combined with solitude—hike the south side of the wilderness and valleys of the Minam and Imnaha Rivers.

Climbing

All peaks have walk-up sides. Some faces look interesting and much of the rock is excellent.

Hiking Season

In a typical June the weather is wet and the highlands under snow. Most years the meadows thaw the first half of July; some rivers then are extremely difficult to ford. July is generally fair and warm. August fair and hot on the average; every third or fourth day is blasted by an afternoon thunderstorm. September is usually cool and clear.

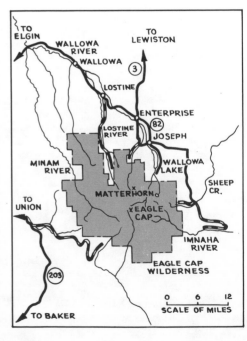

West Fork Wallowa River along Glacier Lake trail

Washington

(Above) Mountain goat beside the Blue Glacier, Olympic National Park
(Opposite) Mt. Johannesburg from side of Eldorado Peak, North Cascades National Park

Paradise Ice Caves, Mt. Rainier National Park

WASHINGTON

1. Olympic National Park
2. Mt. St. Helens—proposed national monument (not fully described in this edition due to total trail closure since the 1980 eruption)
3. Mt. Adams Wilderness
4. Goat Rocks Wilderness
5. Mt. Rainier National Park
6. Cougar Lakes—proposed wilderness
7. Alpine Lakes Wilderness
8. Glacier Peak Wilderness
9. North Cascades National Park
10. Pasayten Wilderness

Other Wilderness (not described)
11. Wenaha-Tucannon

Other Wilderness Study Areas
A. Monte Cristo
B. Boulder Creek
C. Juniper Forest
D. Mt. Bonaparte

Washington offers some of the most varied hiking in the nation—from wilderness ocean beaches to glaciers, from moss-carpeted rain forests to wide-sky semi-deserts.

People once were so few and trails so abundant the encroachment of logging roads scarcely was noticed. Now, though, loggers have chopped up so much wildland, the population has increased so greatly, and so many hikers running out of elbow room in their home states have invaded the Northwest, trails no longer are "in surplus."

The Cascade Range from the Columbia River to Snoqualmie Pass is a green sea of wooded ridges from which thrust the giant volcanoes of St. Helens, Adams, and Rainier and the volcano roots of the Goat Rocks. Snoqualmie Pass marks the boundary of a very different geologic province, the North Cascades, and from here on the range becomes progressively broader, higher, and more sharply glacier-sculptured. The west side of the Cascades is *wet*: late July and early August are generally fair, but even then blue skies cannot be guaranteed. Some years there is no summer at all, just a succession of cold rains between one winter and the next. The east side, the rainshadow, is kinder—frequently, while the west is being drenched, tundras of Chelan and Pasayten country are sun-bright.

A climber never can run out of challenges in Washington. Innumerable "scramble" peaks bridge the gap between trail-walking and difficult climbing. Particularly interesting are the thousands of mixed routes over rock and snow and

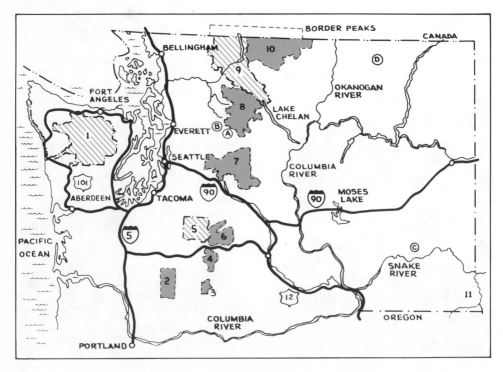

128

ice—truly "alpine" ascents, many short and simple, others long and complex. Containing three-fourths of the glacier area in the old 48, Washington is the ice capital of America—excluding Alaska, of course.

Glacier Peak and Image Lake, Glacier Peak Wilderness

OLYMPIC NATIONAL PARK

Administered by Olympic National Park
Camping permit required
Best season—all year down low, July to Sep-
*   tember up high*
Hiking—excellent
Climbing—poor to fair
Trail map—park handout map is inadequate for
*   hikers*
Guidebooks—102 Hikes in the Alpine Lakes,
*   South Cascades and Olympics, Climber's*
*   Guide to the Olympic Mountains*

Ocean beaches, rain forests, alpine meadows and lakes, glaciers, a maze of peaks, and 600 miles of trails to wander—that's the Olympics.

Though not high—the climax summit, Mt. Olympus, is just 7965 feet—Olympic peaks are tall, rising abruptly from sea level as they do. The large glacier system of Olympus includes the Blue, 2 miles long and nearly 1000 feet thick.

The ocean beach is unique in the 48 conterminous states, containing two 20-mile stretches free from sight or sound of automobiles, exclusively for hiking. However, privacy cannot be expected because this one and only wilderness beach south of Canada is beloved by local hikers and attracts visitors from throughout the nation.

US 101 completely encircles the mountains and for a way follows the ocean shore. Side-roads lead to the various trailheads.

Hiking

Trails typically start in valley forests and follow rivers up to meadows, so hikes generally demand at least two days. Nevertheless, even the center of the range is heavily traveled. One of the most famous and most crowded trails is that of the Hoh River, the first 12 miles in luxuriant rain forest, the next 6 miles ascending to a lovely meadow beside the Blue Glacier and the customary high camp for climbing Olympus. The majority of hikers are content with the first easy miles along the valley bottom.

If the Hoh is mobbed, other rain-forest valleys offer solitude; the Bogachiel is guarded by miles of mud and the Queets is barred to those unable to make the difficult river ford.

Camping permits are required in the national park, which encompasses most of the mountains and wilderness beach. Many trailheads have a "write your own permit" station, but rules change and hikers should check with park headquarters before the trip.

Climbing

Though well-liked by locals, the peaks mainly are of poor rock (shales and sandstones, some basalt) offering mediocre climbing.

Hiking Season

Olympic weather is notoriously bad. Though most of the 12 feet of annual west-slope precipitation falls in winter, summer has a good share. July and August are usually best but even then week-long drizzlings and drenchings are common. The east side of the range is drier, yet far from arid.

Ocean beaches are hikable all year but can be grim in a winter storm. Valley trails such as the Hoh ordinarily are open except for occasional brief snowy periods. Alpine trails do not melt out until early or middle July and are snow-blocked again in late October.

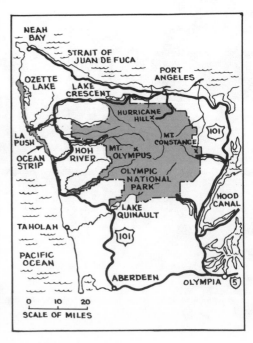

Blue Glacier on Mt. Olympus

MT. ST. HELENS

Administered by Gifford Pinchot National Forest

On May 18, 1980, Mt. St. Helens ceased to be the "Mt. Fuji of the West," one of the most graceful peaks in the nation. However, it did not stop being—as it long had been—one of the most photographed peaks in the nation. In fact, after explosively lowering its summit from 9677 to 8364 feet, it became almost a bore on television and in the newspapers, magazines, and bookstores. But not in person—the new St. Helens is as awesome and exciting a mountain as there is in the nation, and millions of Americans are gathering to gape.

From a distance. Except for scientists and the like studying the volcano, and loggers diminishing the scientific value of the scene by hauling out blast-felled trees, nobody walks on—or anywhere near—St. H, and it may well be that nobody legally will for a dozen years—or 50 years (duration of the last eruptive period, in the 19th century) or 500 years (duration of next to last eruptive period).

Even before the eruption the mountain had been proposed as a national monument—to preserve its remaining forest mantle from the loggers then busy clearcutting to timberline. Now more than ever it deserves such status—to preserve undisturbed an example of 150 square miles recovering from the sort of catastrophe that is, in the deep time of the Cascades, a common occurrence, but the only one that has happened in our shallow time, before our very eyes.

Boundaries of the "Red Zone" and "Blue Zone" around the mountain, within which recreational visits are banned, doubtless will be revised in years ahead, becoming less (or more) restrictive. Current information may be obtained from Gifford Pinchot National Forest.

Impressive views may be obtained from major highways. For the best *hiker's* perspective, go to Mt. Rainier National Park and walk trails above Paradise.

Mt. St. Helens during a minor eruption of April 1981

Tranquil Spirit Lake and Mt. St. Helens before May 18, 1980 eruption

MT. ADAMS WILDERNESS

*Administered by Gifford Pinchot National Forest
and Yakima Indian Reservation*
Wilderness permit required
Best season—early July through mid-October
Trail map—Mt. Adams Wilderness
*Guidebooks—102 Hikes in the Alpine Lakes,
South Cascades and Olympics, Cascade
Alpine Guide*

The small Mt. Adams Wilderness is completely filled and then some by the great bulk of the 12,326-foot volcano, mantled by snowfields and glaciers, meadows and open forests—a lovely land for roaming. The east and southeast of the mountain lie within the Yakima Indian Reservation, mostly managed by the tribe as wilderness. Because areas of equal splendor lie closer to population centers, visitors are comparatively few.

Mt. Adams is located in the southern part of the state, accessible by forest roads either from Randle or Trout Lake. Logging roads are high-grade gravel thoroughfares but some travel is on recreation roads in very poor condition.

Recreation roads extend above forests at Timberline Camp and Bird Creek Meadows. A very interesting lesson is taught by the contrast between eroded hillsides at the former, where livestock once grazed, and lush flower fields of the latter, which were fenced off from domestic herds.

Hiking

Bird Creek Meadows offers easy walks, as does nearby Indian Heaven. The hike to Mountaineer Camp on the northwest side is longer and rougher. The classic trip—for experienced hikers only—is the 43-mile around-the-mountain loop: 28 miles on trail, 15 miles cross-country with several very difficult river crossings.

Climbing

Hikers can attain the top via monotonous slopes of boulders and cinders on the south side. A bit of steep snow makes an ice ax useful, and sometimes crampons. The route starts from 5600-foot Cold Springs Camp and takes one long day.

Climbers prefer the northwest ridge, reached from Killen Creek trail and an overnight stay at 6900-foot Mountaineer Camp. The ascent from the camp is a long, hard day up loose volcanic rock, steep snow, and glaciers; ice ax, rope, and crampons are essential.

Hiking Season

Many ocean-born clouds don't get quite as far as Adams and the weather is sometimes better than elsewhere on the Cascade Crest. The hiking season is limited by the fact access roads seldom are snowfree before July and often are blocked in early fall. The period from mid-July to mid-October is most dependable, but driving conditions at any given time can be learned by calling the Forest Service at Trout Lake.

Mt. Adams from Mountaineer Camp

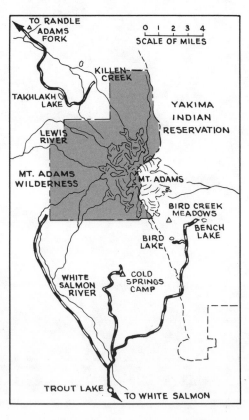

GOAT ROCKS WILDERNESS

*Administered by Gifford Pinchot and Snoqual-
    mie National Forests*
Wilderness permit required
Best season—July through mid-October
Hiking—excellent
Climbing—poor
Trail map—Goat Rocks Wilderness
*Guidebooks—102 Hikes in the Alpine Lakes,
    South Cascades and Olympics, Cascade
    Alpine Guide*

The Goat Rocks Wilderness is a pleasant blend of forests, alpine meadows, snowcovered peaks, and a few glaciers and lakes. Easy trails and gentle terrain draw rather heavy traffic, especially in flower fields around Snowgrass Flat. The highest point of the ancient and deeply-dissected Goat Rocks volcano is 8201-foot Mt. Curtis Gilbert.

Located on the crest of the Cascades between Mt. Rainier and Mt. Adams, the wilderness is readily accessible from US 12 at White Pass and by forest road from Packwood to Packwood Lake, Walupt Lake, or Chambers Lake.

Hiking

The wilderness is traversed by 32 miles of the Pacific Crest Trail, good hiking the whole way. The Pacific Crest Trail rises to one of its two highest stretches in Washington on a 7000-foot ridge of Old Snowy. At spots the path is narrow, blasted from a precipice. Though safe enough for hikers, often there is no room to pass horses, and since animals have the right of way pedestrians must retreat to the nearest turnout.

Among shorter hikes are those to Nanny Ridge and to Snowgrass Flat. The latter has become so popular camping is no longer allowed in the Flat, but carrying a stove permits use of scenic campsites a mile farther up the trail.

Climbing

Most peaks have easy sides and the rock is very poor so climbing is unappealing.

Hiking Season

Trails generally are snowfree early in July, except the Pacific Crest Trail on the side of Old Snowy which may be partly covered until mid-July. Still, horse-passing problems are so severe later in the summer that early July is the best time to hike this section. Snow blocks trails in late October. Weather is somewhat drier than on the Cascade Crest farther north, but the raincoat must not be left home—though sunshine is frequent from July through September, ocean storms do blast in and several hikers have died of hypothermia on the Pacific Crest Trail here.

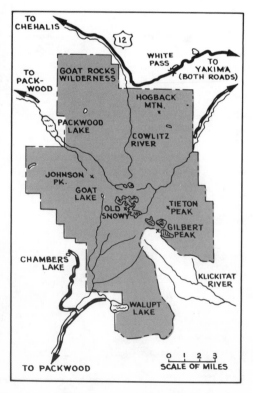

A shoulder of Gilbert Peak

MT. RAINIER NATIONAL PARK

Administered by Mt. Rainier National Park
Camping permits required
Best season—mid-July through September
Hiking—excellent
Climbing—excellent
Trail map—park map is inadequate for hikers
Guidebooks—50 Hikes in Mount Rainier
  National Park, Cascade Alpine Guide

Mt. Rainier, the 14,410-foot granddaddy of Cascade volcanoes and the highest summit within the scope of this book, dominates Puget Sound country. The mountain carries the largest single-peak glacier system in the conterminous 48 states, ice streams radiating from the top like arms of an octopus and flowing far down the slopes on every side. Below the realm of ice are alpine meadows displaying a wildflower climax unsurpassed in the Northwest, and lower still are virgin forests and wild-roaring glacier-fed rivers.

The richly-deserved fame is the mountain's problem, drawing mobs of admirers, mostly so wedded to their cars they won't walk across the parking lot, but enough pedestrians among them to crowd the trails and climbing routes.

Easy access aggravates the problem. A Seattle resident can leave the city in the morning, spend the day roaming gardens or climbing a glacier, and be home for supper. A paved road ascends the south side to 5500-foot Paradise Valley, right in the heart of the meadows. Other roads lead with equal ease to other park beauty spots.

Hiking

Rainier has trails to satisfy any fancy—day hikes through such grand forests as the Grove of the Patriarchs or to such alpine splendors as Klapatche Park and Indian Henrys Hunting Ground, overnighters to the more remote beauties of Mystic Lake or Indian Bar. The 100-mile Wonderland Trail, which completely encircles the mountain, can be done in a sustained effort or in segments of 10-30 miles.

Camping permits are required whether or not a fire is built. Don't be shy about asking rangers for advice; most are ardent back-country rovers and would rather talk to a hiker than a car-enslaved tourist.

Climbing

Of the mountain's numerous climbing routes, some extremely difficult, those via Camp Muir and Steamboat Prow are the most popular. Both entail hauling packs to a 10,000-foot high camp and getting up around midnight for the grueling push to the summit.

All routes involve extended glacier travel. Ice ax, crampons, and rope are mandatory, as are alpine skills, particularly crevasse rescue. Ascents are easiest in June and early July; by August the glaciers are badly crevassed and by September may be impassable.

Hiking Season

The high trails generally are snowfree from mid-July, by which time bridges washed out in spring floods have been replaced, through early October.

Weather is unpredictable, since Rainier not only bears the brunt of every ocean storm but often stirs up its own private squalls. July, August, and early September have the most sunshine but rain or snow can be expected anytime on high trails and drizzles can last a week without break.

Summit climbers often get above lowland clouds, but they may also ascend into a cloud cap and find themselves battling a raging blizzard—the meadows below meanwhile bathed in sun.

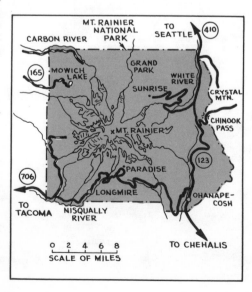

Edith Creek and Mt. Rainier

COUGAR LAKES

*Administered by Wenatchee and Gifford Pinchot
   National Forests*
Best season – June through October
Hiking – excellent
Climbing – none
*Trail map – Snoqualmie National Forest Recrea-
   tion Map is inadequate for hikers*
*Guidebooks – 102 Hikes in the Alpine Lakes,
   South Cascades and Olympics, Cascade
   Alpine Guide*

Friendly country for relaxed hiking in secluded forest valleys, over miles of parkland ridges, by dozens of lakes—that's Cougar Lakes. The area borders Mt. Rainier National Park and on any high walk the great mountain may suddenly and surprisingly pop into view, the massiveness especially impressive in these unexpected encounters. The Pacific Crest Trail traverses the west edge, swinging in and out of the national park.

US 410 crosses Chinook Pass at the north end of the wildland and Highway 12 White Pass at the south end. A paved side-road up the Bumping River from US 410 leads to many trailheads.

Hiking

Legislation to create a Cougar Lakes Wilderness is before Congress; meanwhile the area is administered as wilderness so there is no conflict with machines.

The most popular hike is an easy 4½ miles from Bumping River to Tumac Mountain, an old fire-lookout site; the way passes lovely meadows and one of the Twin Sisters Lakes. Also starting from Bumping River and more strenuous are the 6-mile hike to Cougar Lake and the stern 4000-foot ascent in 6 miles to unlimited views from the summit of Mt. Aix.

Climbing

All peaks have summit trails or easy sides.

Hiking Season

The Cougar Lakes area being in the rainshadow, the weather is tremendously better than on Mt. Rainier a few miles away; clouds typically reach the crest, then shrivel in blue sky. Also, the most easterly trails melt free of snow in early June while those on the crest are buried until July. As is true elsewhere among so many lakes and marshes, the bugfree fall-color season is the pleasantest hiking time.

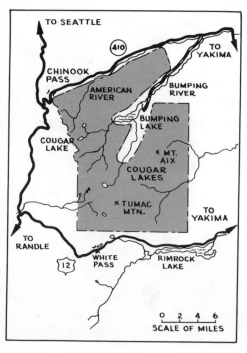

Beargrass on Tumac Mountain, Bismark Peak in distance

ALPINE LAKES WILDERNESS

*Administered by Snoqualmie and Wenatchee
    National Forests*
Best season – July through October
Hiking – excellent
Climbing – excellent
*Trail maps – Forest Service recreation map,
    pictorial relief map*
*Guidebooks – 102 Hikes in the Alpine Lakes,
    South Cascades and Olympics, Cascade
    Alpine Guide*

Magnificent valley forests of Douglas fir and hemlock on the west side, ponderosa pine on the east. Wild rivers tumbling through the trees. An unbelievable number of lakes and tarns in basins gouged by Ice Age glaciers. Dozens of sharp peaks rising from parkland and meadow. Miles and miles of trails for hikers, innumerable cross-country rambles for explorers, and a wealth of walls and pinnacles for climbers.

The proximity of megalopolis means there is mighty little privacy on popular hikes: even off-trail lakes are mobbed.

The Alpine Lakes country extends east from Puget Sound lowlands nearly to the Columbia River, and north from Interstate 90 over Snoqualmie Pass to US 2 over Stevens Pass. Numerous forest roads lead to trailheads.

Hiking

Score of the lakes and peaks lie within reach of easy day hikes, and most can be visited on overnight trips.

The supreme area, the Enchantment Lakes, is defended by an extremely steep and rough trail that climbs 5400 feet from the Icicle River and demands a minimum three days just to get in and out, not to mention roaming-around time. Despite rigors of the approach the other-world granite basins are crowded, especially during fall-color season.

No consensus ever could be gained for the second-greatest trip. LaBohn Gap, reached from the Middle Fork Snoqualmie River, would get a lot of votes, but so would Copper Lake, reached from the Foss River, and Rachel Lake, from the Kachess River, and Deep Lake, from the Cle Elum River, and Ingalls Lake from the North Fork Teanaway River.

Climbing

The Alpine Lakes wildland was the nursery of modern mountaineering in Washington and continues to serve as the local training ground for Seattle-Tacoma. Climbers can begin with easy scrambles and progress to steep rock and snow and perhaps eventually pioneer a route up a virgin granite wall in the Cashmere Crags of the Enchantment Lakes area.

Mt. Stuart, at 9415 feet the second-highest nonvolcanic peak in the Cascades, is a delightful scramble via the east ridge, a memorable Class 3-4 tour by the west ridge, a major challenge by the north cliffs and glaciers.

Hiking Season

Straddling the Cascade Crest, the Alpine Lakes country has a maritime climate on the west, rainshadow climate on the east. Though clouds are not unremitting on west slopes throughout the summer, and indeed some years the sky is blue weeks at a time in July and August, Puget Sound hikers quickly learn that ocean fogs and drizzles frequently can be escaped by dodging across the crest. Of course, rain comes to the east, too, but not as often and not as much.

Virtually every low valley has been logged and roaded, so there is sadly little spring walking. High trails usually are passable early in July, with only a few snowpatches, and stay open through October. However, many lakes do not melt out until mid-July or August and some years not at all.

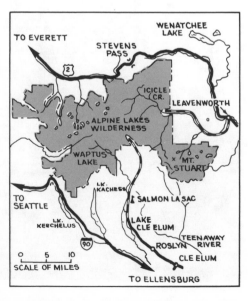

Prusik Peak and Gnome Tarn

GLACIER PEAK WILDERNESS

Administered by Mt. Baker and Wenatchee National Forests
Wilderness permit required
Best season – mid-July to mid-October
Hiking – excellent
Climbing – excellent
Trail map – Glacier Peak Wilderness
Guidebooks – 101 Hikes in the North Cascades, Cascade Alpine Guide

Here is the beginning of the quintessential North Cascades — cathedral forests in deep valleys, loud waterfalls and brawling rivers, high ridges bright with flowers, raw moraines and vivid blue lakes, tall and craggy peaks thrusting above vast glaciers. Not dominating its neighbors but rather ruling as first among equals is Washington's only true wilderness volcano, 10,528-foot Glacier Peak. At the foot of the wildland on the east is the unique inland fiord of Lake Chelan.

Large though it is, the wilderness encompasses merely a fraction of the splendors deserving protection and conservationists are working to have Congress push out the boundaries on every side. They are also striving to prevent Kennecott Copper from desecrating the heart of the area with an open-pit mine.

The Glacier Peak Wilderness extends from near Stevens Pass to the North Cascades National Park. Access is from forest roads leading inward from Puget Sound on the west, Columbia River on the east, and by trails from Lake Chelan.

Hiking

A few of the many trails are crowded but others are so rarely walked the tread is lost in flowers and heather; solitude is easily gained on off-trail wanders.

Day hikers can sample forests of the Suiattle and White Chuck Rivers; they can attain high gardens on Meadow Mountain, reached by a 3-mile trail from the White Chuck, and Green Mountain, also 3 miles from the Suiattle. However, the inner vastnesses require trips of from overnight to five to nine days.

The most popular hike is to Image Lake, 15 miles from the Suiattle road, right next to Kennecott's proposed mine. The view of Glacier Peak across the waters of the lake and the fringing meadows and the deep gulf of the Suiattle valley is world-famous. Other favorites are Buck Creek Pass, 10 miles from the Chiwawa River road, and

Meander Meadows, 6 miles from the Little Wenatchee River trailhead.

The Pacific Crest Trail traverses the wilderness and one of its loveliest sections is the stretch from Stevens Pass to Glacier Peak, winding for miles through parkland and meadows.

Climbing

Glacier Peak offers routes from easy to quite difficult; all are mainly on glaciers (of course) and require rope, ice ax, and usually crampons. Most ascents are via the White Chuck River and the southwest shoulder, a strenuous two days.

Dome Peak, with broad glaciers and sharp spires of sound granite, accessible only to the wilderness mountaineer, is the favorite of the connoisseurs, though. Formidable Tenpeak, and others have their fans, as does 9511-foot Bonanza, highest nonvolcanic peak in the Cascades.

The classic high alpine tour is the Ptarmigan Traverse, strictly for strong, experienced climbers, crossing glaciers, moraines, high cols, and steep mountainsides from Cascade Pass south to Dome Peak, demanding a week or more if any peaks are to be ascended on the way

Climbers are asked to sign in and out at the nearest ranger station. Each station has a register book at the front entrance, available day and night.

Hiking Season

The west side of the wilderness receives very heavy precipitation, as can be guessed from the

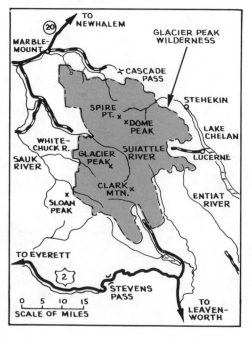

lushness of valley jungles and the size of the glaciers; some years nearby Verlot leads the old 48 states in annual rainfall. Years without a summer are common, though at the worst a week or two of sunshine usually break the gray procession of storms, and occasionally mid-July to mid-August is steadily bright with just a few spells of mist and drizzle. In bad years wily hikers transfer their affections to the east side of the wilderness, the rainshadow country, which is far from bone-dry but gets a lot more sun than windward slopes.

Some valleys are open in April or May and a few high eastern routes melt free of snow in mid-June but most alpine trails are buried deep until mid-July, and again after mid-October.

Deer near White Rock Lake, Dome Peak in distance

NORTH CASCADES NATIONAL PARK

Administered by North Cascades National Park
Camping permit required
Best season—mid-July to mid-October
Hiking—excellent (but rugged)
Climbing—excellent
Trail map—North Cascades National Park
*Guidebooks—***101 Hikes in the North Cascades,***
  Cascade Alpine Guide, Stehekin

The climax of the Cascade Range starts in the Glacier Peak Wilderness and culminates in the North Cascades National Park, the country there even rougher and colder. Ancient glaciers trenched the valleys deep and plucked the peaks sharp, and the sculpture continues—it's a rare mountain of any size without glaciers little or large. Here and there meadows relieve the austerity. Below the cliffs and ice are green hills of alder, and lower still, majestic forests.

As established in 1968 the park is pitifully small measured against the opportunity, omitting more magnificence (Mt. Baker, for example) than it includes, and conservationists therefore are working toward at least tripling the acreage.

The North Cascades National Park and the associated Ross Lake and Lake Chelan National Recreation Areas extend to the Canadian border. Access is from the Mt. Baker Highway, North Cascades Highway, forest roads up the Baker and Cascade Rivers, and by boat on Ross Lake and Lake Chelan.

Hiking

Though plentiful, trails in general are long and/or rugged. A notable exception is the 6½-mile supertrail to Cascade Pass, unquestionably among the most spectacular (and busy) paths in the Northwest; crowds thin out and views grow bigger another 2 miles up Sahale Arm. The staggering panorama from Sourdough Mountain does not have to be shared with a throng—the 6000 feet gained by the trail in 6½ miles from Diablo guarantee that.

It is mandatory to walk the Big Beaver valley from Ross Lake to beaver ponds and groves of huge cedars, and the Thunder Creek valley from Diablo Lake into awesome forests of fir and hemlock. Seattle City Light wants to drown both valleys for a few kilowatts; conservationists vow it never will happen.

Steep valley walls and wicked brush make the ordinary traveler content to stay on trails. The dedicated bushwhacker, though, can attain dreamlovely and absolutely-lonesome ridgetop gardens.

Climbing

The granite towers of Liberty Bell rise from the North Cascades Highway blasted in their base, but ascents more typically are over a combination of rock and ice after a grueling approach on trail and through brush. The wilderness mountaineer reaching tops of famous peaks in such areas as the Pickets and the Redoubt group may find his are the first boots there in several years. Cascade Pass is the busiest climbing center, the mountains large and magnificent and the approaches requiring minimum time and struggle.

The companion giants, 10,778-foot Baker, a volcano almost completely white with ice, and 9127-foot Shuksan, whose standard route is a stimulating mix of rock-scrambling and glacier travel, have trails to the basecamps and are climbed by hundreds of people annually. Both offer very stern challenges in addition to the easiest routes.

Hiking Season

The 300-odd glaciers in the park speak eloquently of the sort of weather to expect. On any day of any month the highlands can be swept by a blizzard and the typical summer has many more rainy days (or snowy) than sunny. The best chances of not getting drenched or frozen are from mid-July through August, and sometimes

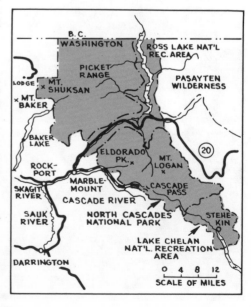

September. Still, the Stehekin area and the adjoining Chelan Crest are in the rainshadow, frequently offering escapes from gray.

The trails up Big Beaver and Thunder Creeks are open in May, as are those of Agnes Creek and the Baker River. The high trails usually are deep in white until mid-July and partly blocked all summer. Snow can bury the meadows from mid-September on, the average being mid-October.

Hikers on shoulder of Eldorado Peak

PASAYTEN WILDERNESS

Administered by Okanogan National Forest
Wilderness permit required
Best season—mid-June through October
Hiking—excellent
Climbing—very little
Trail map—Pasayten Wilderness
*Guidebooks—**101 Hikes in the North Cascades,**
Cascade Alpine Guide*

Is this really and truly the Cascades? Roaming enormous tundras, far and away the largest in the range, a hiker may wonder if he has not somehow strayed north to the Arctic. Glaciers and craggy peaks are fewer and the entire aspect milder than in country westward, but the joys are no less sweet amid miles and miles of parkland and flowers. And the weather is infinitely better and the trail population tiny.

The Pasayten Wilderness, 52 miles across, seems even bigger because of the North Cascades National Park to the west, de facto wilderness adjoining on the north in Canada, and de facto wildlands of Chopaka Mountain east and Chewack River south. Conservationists in two nations are working to convert "de facto" to "statutory."

Access on the west is from Ross Lake, in the center from the North Cascades Highway via forest roads to 6200-foot Harts Pass and to Billy Goat Corral, and on the east from the Okanogan valley via a forest road up Toats Coulee Creek to 6000-foot Iron Gate Camp.

Hiking

The wilderness has an extensive trail system and off-trail exploring is easy and superb. Just about the only short trips, though, are the 3-mile saunter from Harts Pass through gardens along the Pacific Crest Trail to Windy Pass, and the 5-mile walk from Iron Gate Camp into the broad parks and tundras of Horseshoe Basin.

The Pasayten is particularly delightful to long-distance backpackers. The Devils Dome-Devils Park-Crater Mountain loop from Ross Lake samples the west part of the wilderness in a glorious week. The Pacific Crest Trail north from Harts Pass is continuously high and exciting. The Boundary Trail traversing the north edge of the wilderness from Iron Gate to Ross Lake provides a two-week return to an earlier, lonesomer era.

Climbing

Most of the mountains have walk-up sides. One exception is 8928-foot Jack, rising high and mighty from Ross Lake. Another is the South Tower of Hozomeen, standing above the Skagit close to the Canadian border. There are a few other challenges, but the climber finds more and better sport south of the wilderness on the granite of 8876-foot Silver Star and adjacent pinnacles.

Hiking Season

The west part of the wilderness is rainshadowed by ranges of North Cascades National Park and thus is much less snowy and rainy than the formidable Pickets. The east part is doubly and triply rainshadowed and virtually arid. The farther east, the better the weather. July, August, and September are mostly blue sky months with occasional rain squalls or afternoon thundershowers.

Tundra trails open as early as Memorial Day in the east, the end of June in the west, and rarely are blocked by snow before November. The contrast with the "typical" North Cascades is striking.

Louden Lake in Horseshoe Basin

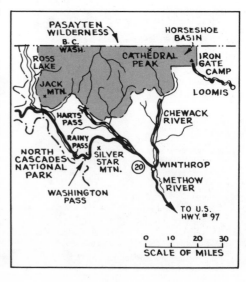

148

British Columbia

(Above) Ptarmigan, Tantalus Range
(Opposite) Homathko Icefield in the Coast Range

Black Tusk Meadows, Garibaldi National Park

BRITISH COLUMBIA

1. Sapper, Skagit, E.C. Manning, and Cathedral Lakes Provincial Parks
2. Pacific Rim National Park
3. Strathcona Provincial Park
4. Garibaldi and Golden Ears Provincial Parks
5. Tantalus Range–Lillooet Mountains
6. Coast Range
7. Monashee Mountains–Cariboo Mountains
8. Glacier and Mt. Revelstoke National Parks
9. Purcell Range

By Canadian standards the lower United States has hardly any true wilderness, few real mountains, and mere snippets of ice. British Columbia is nearly as large as Washington, Oregon, Idaho, and Montana combined and half its 2,000,000 people live in and around the single city of Vancouver, meaning there is an awful lot of empty country. Coverage here is limited to the more famous areas in the southern third of the province, omitting innumerable others that if located below the 49th Parallel would be widely publicized and heavily traveled.

These are principally *northern* ranges with enormous glaciers, brief summers, and weather varying from poor to impossible. A good share of the continent's grandest peaks are in British Columbia and adjacent Alberta, many offering ice and rock challenges to test the most daring alpinist, some accessible to none but the expedition mountaineer. Hiking opportunities, though magnificent, are restricted by the current rarity of easy trails; except in several parks, hikers are not pampered the way they are south of the border. The B.C. Forest Service, unlike the U.S. Forest Service, does not see recreation as one of its responsibilities and has abandoned trails once needed for administration, using roads and airplanes instead.

The conservation ethic is barely beginning to prick the consciousness of government officials. Huge regions of matchless natural glories lack any protection at all and "belong" absolutely to loggers and miners—and dammers who for the sake of electricity have perpetrated some of the most destructive floods (permanent, not temporary) since the one that made Noah a sailor. Park status means less in Canada than in the United States, considerable commercial exploitation being allowed and the boundaries subject to casual revision. Wildernesses guaranteed by statute are few and "nature conservancies" protected by administrative regulation scarce. Recreationists are doing their share to dilute the wildness—heavens that would demand many harrowing days to attain on foot are cheapened by quicky-vacationers using floatplane and helicopter to plop down at the very poles of remoteness. However, the times are changing, citizens are rebelling against the reckless past, and government is starting to respond. Americans must pray Canadians move swiftly to protect their land from ruthless exploitation (American corporations being the worst offenders) and to preserve and restore their wild heritage so that together with that of Alaska it will in future provide people of the continent and earth a chance of weeks-from-anywhere solitude.

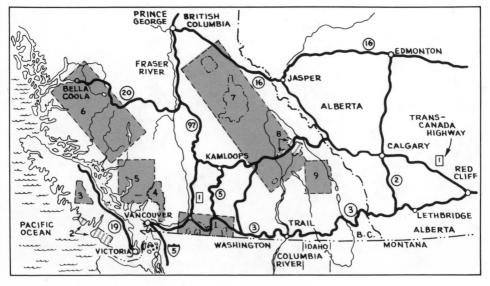

Snowpatch Spire and Bugaboo Glacier from Frenchman Mountain trail, Purcell Range

SAPPER, SKAGIT, E.C. MANNING, AND CATHEDRAL LAKES PROVINCIAL PARKS

Administered by B.C. Parks Branch and B.C.
Forest Service
Best season — July through October
Hiking — excellent
Climbing — some
Trail map — park brochures
Guidebooks — 103 Hikes in Southwestern Brit-
ish Columbia, Alpine Guide to Southwestern
British Columbia, Exploring Manning Park

The portions of the North Cascades in Canada share the character of neighboring areas across the 49th Parallel. In the west the startling fang of Mt. Slesse is the most frightening of the Border Peaks, and the Cheam Range (Lucky Four Group) leaps with forbidding abruptness from the Fraser River. Sapper Park, which includes part of Chilliwack Lake — a genuine lake (not a reservoir) that resembles the head of Lake Chelan — is a natural extension of North Cascades National Park. Skagit Park encompasses a sample of the last free-running section of the upper Skagit River. E.C. Manning and Cathedral Parks contain tundras as vast and marvelous as those in the adjacent Pasayten Wilderness.

The existing provincial parks cover only a little of the climax country and conservationists therefore are proposing major expansions. They further are developing plans to assemble a grand Salish National Park preserving British Columbia splendors and guarding wildness on the American side.

Access to the western British Columbia Cascades is by forest roads from Highway 401, to the center from Highway 3 crossing the range at 4436-foot Allison Pass, and to the east by forest roads from Highway 3.

Hiking

The few western trails mostly are too rough to be recommended; Chilliwack Lake, though, offers an easy look at the land. From Sardis on Highway 401 drive about 30 miles on forest road to the lake and continue 10 miles along the shore to the lakehead campground, admiring cliffs rising from the 2100-foot waters to small glaciers on 6000-7000-foot peaks. Hike a primitive trail into green-gloomy cedar and hemlock forests along Dolly Varden Creek, or a steep, crude 3-mile path to 4700-foot Hanging Lake.

E.C. Manning Park is an exception to the rule that "there ain't no trails in British Columbia, just bushwhackers' routes." A number of paths lead to forest lakes, alpine lakes, and meadows. A fire-access road (closed to private cars) leaves Highway 3 at the tourist center 5 miles east of Allison Pass and in 4½ miles climbs 2200 feet to the 5987-foot parkland summit of Windy Joe Mountain. At 2½ miles up the fire road a trail branches off 8 miles to the top of the highest peak in the park, 7900-foot Mt. Frosty; the final slopes are something of a scramble but the flower gardens and views south into Pasayten Wilderness are reward enough even if the summit is foregone. The most popular hike is the Heather Trail. From the tourist center east of Allison Pass drive Blackwall Peak road 8 miles to its end at about 6300 feet. The trail (on fire road the first 3 miles) wanders 14 miles over tundra ridges flanking Three Brothers Mountain (highest peak, 7453 feet), flowers all the way and endless views, at the end descending to Nicomen Lake.

Cathedral Lakes, set in cirques beneath granite walls of Cathedral Peak, are reached by a 6-mile forest road leaving Highway 3 about 6 miles east of Keremeos, then a 9-mile private jeep road; jeep

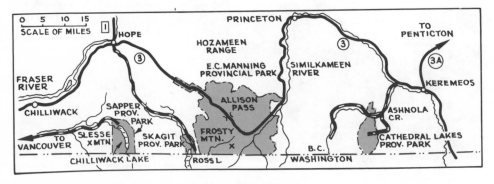

154

service is provided by Cathedral Lakes Resort. Walk the lake trails or roam upward into meadows.

Climbing

All but a few peaks in Cathedral Lakes and E.C. Manning Parks have walk-up sides and the remainder require only scrambling. Several of the Lucky Four Group offer interesting ascents on broken glaciers, steep snow, and highly-mineralized, crumbly rock. The supreme challenge of the region is 8000-foot Mt. Slesse, reached by the Vedder-Chilliwack road from Sardis on Highway 401 and then 7 rough and tough miles up Slesse Creek logging road. The trail climbs a murderous 5000 feet in 3 miles to a 6500-foot high camp under the spire, whose cliffs are strictly for experts.

Hiking Season

The western part receives heavy winter snows and rain most of the summer. Chilliwack Lake is open for walking in May but the high country is white until mid-July. Manning Park and country eastward are in the rainshadow, trails usually open in early July, summer weather mostly sunny, and snow not a big problem until late October.

Air view of Mt. Slesse

PACIFIC RIM NATIONAL PARK

Administered by Pacific Rim National Park
Best season—June to September
Hiking—good
Climbing—none
Trail map—unknown
*Guidebook—*The West Coast Trail and Nitinat Lakes

Since 1854 at least 60 ships attempting to enter the Strait of Juan de Fuca have been driven by storms onto the stretch of Vancouver Island's west coast called the Graveyard of the Pacific. Subsequent to the 1906 wreck of the *S.S. Valencia* which killed 126 people, in 1909 the federal government built the Life Saving Trail so unfortunate mariners lucky enough to get ashore could escape the rough wilderness on foot. Though new rescue methods ultimately eliminated need for the trail, recreational hikers now have discovered beauties of the 50-mile route, which partly follows beach, partly beats through forest jungle.

In 1970 the Life Saving trail, or West Coast trail, together with a buffer strip of virgin forest, was placed in a Pacific Rim National Park, the first national park on Canada's west coast. Other units of the park are Long Beach, south of Tofino, with a few short trails, and the Broken Group Islands, a kayaker's delight.

The north end of the trail at Bamfield is reached by private road from Port Alberni, or by the ferry, *Lady Rose*, from Port Alberni. The south end at Port Renfrew is reached by road from Victoria or Duncan. The midpoint at Nitinat Lake (a superb tidal lake amid lush forest) is reached by road from Port Alberni, then down-lake boat service supplied by Indians of the Nitinat Band.

Long Beach is paralleled by the road to Tofino from Port Alberni.

Hiking

Though thousands of people annually hike the entire West Coast trail and many others visit the ends and middle, the trip is no simple beach walk, requires an average 7-9 days for the full 50 miles, and should be attempted only by experienced wilderness travelers. Deep ravines must be crossed on old and treacherous bridges, streams must be rafted or swum, and dangers abound in forest chasms and on beach cliffs. Ropes should be carried for belaying over swift rivers, slippery footlogs, and steep rock, plus a supply of large nails and stout nylon cord for building driftwood rafts. A tide table is essential for planning passages around headlands. Some difficulties may be eliminated in future, though there is strong feeling the route should be left strenuous and thus wild.

However, beaches and forests of the north section can be visited easily and safely if a party turns back when the going gets spooky. Rain forests of Nitinat Lake are richly worth a trip in their own right. The trail from Bamfield starts at Pachena Bay Indian village. The first 6 miles to Pachena Point Lighthouse is through dense forest on a supertrail—which beyond the lighthouse quickly deteriorates. For a modest fee, a sometimes-there-and-sometimes-not Nitinat ferry takes hikers across the swift stream at the outlet of Nitinat Lake.

Climbing—None

Hiking Season

The trail is open all year but the fall-winter-spring storms that make this the Graveyard of the Pacific are equally brutal to hikers. High water from heavy rains or spring snowmelt in the Vancouver Island mountains can render streams impassable by any means. Summer is the kindest season and even then one must expect more rain and fog than sunshine.

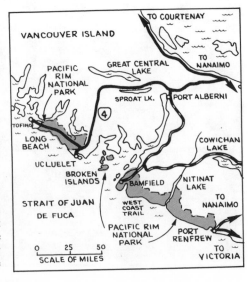

Pachena Point Lighthouse

STRATHCONA PROVINCIAL PARK

Administered by Strathcona Provincial Park
Best season – July through October
Hiking – good
Climbing – fair
Trail map – Strathcona Provincial Park
Guidebooks – 103 Hikes in Southwestern Brit-
  ish Columbia, Climber's Guide to the
  Coastal Ranges of British Columbia

Strathcona offers one of the very few large examples of low-elevation climax forest preserved in British Columbia, a wonderland of alpine lakes and ridges, sharp little peaks decorated by glaciers, and panoramas over the Strait of Georgia to ice giants of the mainland Coast Range.

Vancouver Island currently is being clearcut with a ruthlessness American timber companies (which are doing most of the job) have not been permitted in their own nation for 40 years. Strathcona Park is the only extensive area set aside from the great rape; even there protection is less than perfect, since some logging is allowed in Canadian parks. The rest of the Vancouver Island mountains, including country once as lovely as that in the park wilderness, is riddled by private logging roads gradually being opened to the public, which at last is beginning to realize how its heritage has been devastated.

Strathcona Park, located at the center of the island, is easily accessible from Highway 19.

Hiking

Except in the park, island trails are few and neglected. Dense timber and formidable brush pretty well rule out off-trail travel down low but above 4000 feet the jungle yields to meadows delightful for cross-country rambles.

The most famous attraction of the park is *Forbidden Plateau*, a wide ridge with lakes, heather fields, and easily-climbed peaks. From Courtenay on Highway 19 drive 14 miles to the 2000-foot road-end ski resort. The trail, possibly unmarked, the first part following an abandoned road, climbs 3 miles to 4538-foot Mt. Becher and broad views, then continues a dozen miles along the ridge, offering enough explorations for a week. A mandatory side-trip is to the Rock Garden above McKenzie Lake.

Flower Ridge. From the road on the shore of almost sea level Buttle Lake, reached from Campbell River on Highway 19, the trail climbs some 4000 feet in 5 miles to the ridgetop and glorious walking through miles of red and white heather, past countless tarns ranging from footbath-size to family tubs. Experienced off-trail navigators can continue along connecting ridges for days of wildland wandering.

Climbing

The peaks, not high but rugged, generally are walks or scrambles. However, a number offer interesting short routes on glaciers, steep snow, and mainly mediocre rock. Despite encroachment of logging roads, some still are wilderness mountains, requiring lengthy cross-country approaches. The highest and second-highest peaks on Vancouver Island, 7219-foot Golden Hinde and 7190-foot Elkhorn Mountain, are among the favorite climbs.

Hiking Season

Enough snow usually is melted away in early July to allow hiking; deep whiteness is not a problem again until late October. Weather is typical of mountains so close to the ocean, which is to say, terrible. Some summers the rain never quits and the catch-22 is that when the sun shines very long the region is closed to travel on account of forest fire danger.

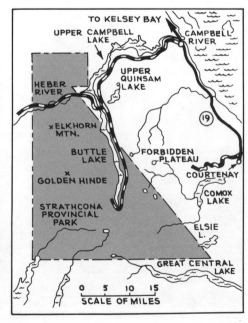

Mt. Septimus and tarn on Flower Ridge

GARIBALDI AND GOLDEN EARS PROVINCIAL PARKS

Administered by Garibaldi Provincial Park
Best season—mid-July to October
Hiking—excellent
Climbing—good
Trail maps—Garibaldi Provincial Park, Golden
  Ears Provincial Park
Guidebooks—103 Hikes in Southwestern Brit-
  ish Columbia, Climber's Guide to the
  Coastal Ranges of British Columbia, Explor-
  ing Garibaldi Park

Garibaldi contains turquoise lakes and cascading streams, forests and meadows, glaciers and icecaps, lava flows and mountains—not the highest but certainly the most famous being 8787-foot Mt. Garibaldi, an old and deeply dissected volcano.

A small part of the park is in the Black Tusk Nature Conservancy, maintained as wilderness, and a larger section is so remote as to be visited only by experienced mountaineers on week-long cross-country hikes. Other portions are developed for tourists. Adjoining the park on the southeast is Golden Ears Provincial Park, extending from low-elevation lakes to highlands.

Garibaldi Park is easily accessible from Highway 99 running north of Vancouver along picturesque Howe Sound, Golden Ears from Haney on Highway 7 east of Vancouver.

Hiking

Garibaldi Park is the most popular hiking area near Vancouver, mainly because it has one of the few good trail systems in the region. Diamond Head, Garibaldi Lake, and Black Tusk Meadows swarm with humanity and new roads and trails surely will make Mamquam Lake equally crowded.

Camping is restricted to designated places; at some, wood fires are banned. Hikers and climbers visiting the back country must register in Squamish either at the park's branch office or headquarters of the Royal Canadian Mounted Police.

Diamond Head. Hike an abandoned jeep road to overlooks of the lovely tarns of Elfin Lakes; the public campground is nearby. From Highway 99 north of Squamish drive the Ring River road, then a steep logging road to a gate at 3300 feet. Walk 7 miles to the site of an old chalet at 5000 feet The trail leads through meadows past the

Gargoyles, weird volcanic towers, to 7000-foot Diamond Head and views of the broad Garibaldi Névé (icecap).

Garibaldi Lake-Black Tusk Meadows. A long day hike, or better overnight or a full week. From Highway 99 at Garibaldi Station drive the short Rubble Creek road to the 2000-foot end. The trail ascends 2500 feet in 4 forest miles to a junction. The left fork goes 1½ miles, passing Taylor Creek Campground, to 5500-foot Black Tusk Meadows. The right fork drops 1½ miles to Garibaldi Lake, nice camps, and a 1½-mile trail climbing to Black Tusk Meadows. From the meadow junction of the two approach trails a rough and at times steep path proceeds some 2½ miles to a tremendous viewpoint at 7400 feet on Panorama Ridge; Mimulus Lake, Black Tusk Lake, Helm Lake, and Cinder Flats are easy side-trips.

Climbing

Climbers must register at Garibaldi Lake Ranger Station or Diamond Head Chalet. Of the many good climbs, some requiring days-long

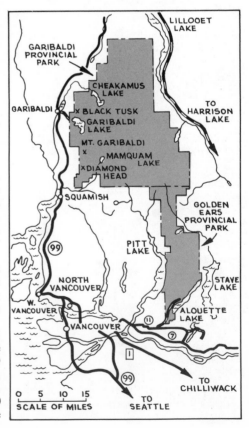

160

approaches, the best-known are Black Tusk and Mt. Garibaldi.

Black Tusk, 7598 feet. The volcanic plug is an easy flower scramble from Black Tusk Meadows to the face of the Tusk, then a Class 3 climb up a rotten chimney. The actual summit is a pinnacle separated from the main peak by a 30-foot-deep chasm, involving a rappel to the bottom and a Class 4 climb to the top.

Mt. Garibaldi, 8787 feet. Reached either from Diamond Head or Garibaldi Lake, the latter route requiring a boat ride or a difficult cross-country hike to Table Bay. Ascent of the very steep glacier is rather easy or virtually impossible, depending on crevasse conditions.

Hiking Season

The large glaciers testify to the heavy snowfall. Alpine trails usually are clear by mid-July and open through October. Flowers are at their best in mid-August. Summer weather is fair to miserable, some years mainly sunny with only a few weeks of steady rain, others steadily gray and wet with only brief bright spells.

Mt. Garibaldi and Garibaldi Lake

TANTALUS RANGE–
LILLOOET MOUNTAINS

Administered by B.C. Forest Service
Fire permit required
Best season–July to mid-October
Hiking–Tantalus Range poor, Lillooet Mountains fair
Climbing–Tantalus Range excellent, Lillooet Mountains fair
Trail maps–unknown
*Guidebooks–*103 Hikes in Southwestern British Columbia, Climber's Guide to the Coastal Ranges of British Columbia

Here, less than 50 miles from Vancouver, the northland begins. Glaciers and cliffs of the Tantalus Range and icefields of the Lillooet Mountains are visible from Garibaldi Park summits and even the highway, yet belong more properly to the realm of expeditions than ordinary hiking and climbing. However, those willing and able to make the effort gain a wilderness experience no longer to be found below the border.

Road access is from Highway 99 past Howe Sound to Pemberton and from Highway 1 up the Fraser River. For a cheaper experience (in quality, not cash) see the climber's guide concerning airplane access.

Hiking

Hikers and climbers must register with the Royal Canadian Mounted Police and obtain a fire permit from the B.C. Forest Service, both in Squamish.

Tantalus Range

The average hiker will gasp at the highway view—and then head for Garibaldi Park. Entry is complicated and trails few and cross-country travel strictly for bush-apes and climbers.

One of the rare trails leads to 3850-foot Lake Lovely Water under the southeast buttress of 8450-foot Mt. Tantalus, highest peak in the range. Drive north of Squamish several miles to Cheekye, cross the Cheakamus River, and ask at one of the first three houses for an Indian willing to ferry the party (for a fee) over the Squamish River to the trail. The lake is reached by some four hours of hard labor. Rough paths (routes, really) ascend from the lake to small meadows, moraines, and big glaciers.

Those who hike there will be sorry to hear the lake is also accessible by floatplane.

Lillooet Mountains

Most of the grand sprawl of glaciers and mountains centered on the Lillooet River is beyond the grasp of the average hiker but a few rough trails, including that to Tenquille Lake, give splendid samplings. From Pemberton drive Lillooet River road about 15 miles to the 1000-foot trailhead. The path starts in steep forest and in 7 miles climbs to the 5200-foot alpine lake and large meadows.

Climbing

Glaciers and granite of the Tantalus Range provide the finest rock and ice climbing near Vancouver. Mt. Tantalus usually is ascended from Lake Lovely Water.

Though some approach 10,000 feet, most of the Lillooet Mountains are snow walks and/or rock scrambles; those in the east are mainly rounded humps. But the remoteness in itself excites climbers and huge glaciers of the western part offer arctic-like journeys and excellent ice routes. Lillooet Icecap demands arduous bushwhacking and torrent-fording from the Lillooet River road.

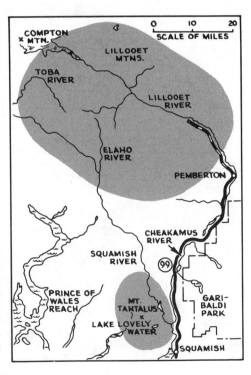

Hiking Season

Tantalus weather is as bad or worse than that of Garibaldi Park. What trails there are usually melt out by mid-July; Lake Lovely Water may remain frozen weeks longer.

The western Lillooets are as stormy as the Tantalus but the east side is in the rainshadow, with better weather and the high country open enough for hiking in early July—though routes with rivers to ford are impassable until August.

Lillooet River and peaks of the Coast Range

COAST RANGE

Administered by B.C. Forest Service
Best season—July and August
Hiking—little
Climbing—excellent
Trail map—unknown
*Guidebook—***Climber's Guide to the Coastal
Ranges of British Columbia**

The mile-high summits rising steeply from salt-water to form the northern "city limits" of Vancouver are impressive enough, but scarcely suggest what lies beyond the metropolitan skyline in the 800-mile length of the British Columbia Coast Range to its merger with the St. Elias Mountains of Yukon Territory and Alaska. Garibaldi, Tantalus Range and Lillooet Mountains are the prelude. The climax is 13,104-foot Mt. Waddington, highest in the range and except for St. Elias peaks highest in the province.

Some of the world's worst weather feeds enormous icecaps that bury all but the tallest thrusts of sharp-plucked rock, and nourishes the most infamous brush jungles of the continent, and swells the rivers to steady-roaring torrents. Glaciers of the even colder past gouged deep valleys walled by formidable cliffs and dug the saltwater-filled fiords that equal in majesty any on earth. The rainshadowed east slope is drier and sunnier, actually quite kindly, but though lacking violent drama is sufficiently rough to forbid easy entry.

This huge mountain system is given short notice here because difficulties of access keep it in the domain of the expedition climber and the adventurous hiker. The situation is changing rapidly as logging roads advance (apparently every commercially-valuable stand of trees is doomed) and perhaps in a few years ordinary climbers and hikers will crowd the area.

Suggesting ways to a wilderness undergoing such swift attrition would not be helpful. Visits to inner fastnesses nowadays are facilitated (if cheapened) by airplanes; see the climber's guide.

Hiking

It is not true there are *no* trails in the Coast Range, but there certainly are few the average hiker would consider comfortable. Infinite joys await in the high country—meadowlands, open ridges, alpine lakes, and dazzling views—once good trails are built, as they will be when national parks are established. The wildness will diminish then, of course, but at the same time will gain guarantees for the future it totally lacks now.

By local inquiry at Bella Coola, Chilko Lake, Lake Tatlayoko, and other villages and settlements a prowling hiker can learn which trappers' or fishermen's paths currently are thought to be reasonably passable, and how to find them.

Climbing

The super-alpine Coast Range is a paradise for the cold-blooded mountaineer. Much of the climbing (and camping as well) is on smooth icecaps and fractured glaciers. The rock, largely but not entirely granite and varying from excellent to rotten, normally is coated by a certain amount of verglas or snow or frost feathers. Many peaks are easy once the strenuous approach is completed, even simple walk-ups in snow or over heather and boulders. Others are as stern as any in the Western Hemisphere.

Mt. Waddington, until the 1930s so obscured by clouds and rumor as to be called "Mystery Mountain," its location disputed and its very existence widely doubted, has become a "popular" climb. The usual approach is by float-

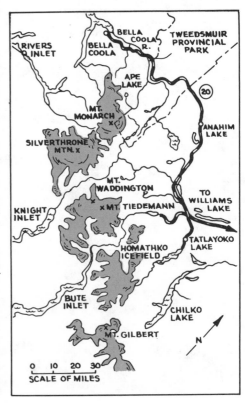

plane to Ghost Lake or Ephemeron Lake, a short, rough walk to tarns and heather gardens of Nabob Pass, then a long slog over the Tiedemann Glacier. The final ascent is up a steep, badly-crevassed glacier and mixed ice and rock of the summit tower.

Hiking Season

The crest knows a single season, winter. During any given week of any given "summer" a party has about a 50 percent chance of one or two sunny days sandwiched between days-long blizzards and snow-fogs. Suspicions have been expressed that climbers go to the Coast Range not for derring-do but for a good, long sleep. The eastern rain-shadow is a different story; when trails are built to the beauty spots they quickly will be mobbed.

Air view of Mt. Waddington and the Scimitar Glacier

MONASHEE MOUNTAINS– CARIBOO MOUNTAINS

Administered by B.C. Parks Branch and B.C. Forest Service
Best season–June through October
Hiking–limited
Climbing–excellent
Trail maps–unknown
*Guidebook–***Climber's Guide to the Interior Ranges of British Columbia**

Noble peaks and grand icefields mark some of the most pristine wilderness of British Columbia, until the age of the cheap chopper, unknown to hikers and all but a few climbers. An essentially single range is divided by the North Thompson River, the area to the south called the Monashee Mountains, to the north the Cariboo Mountains.

Though crossed by Highway 1, foot access is difficult to the Monashees, trails being virtually nonexistent and brush fierce. Views from the city of Revelstoke include 8936-foot Mt. Begbie and its small glacier, and the highest point in the range, the snow dome of 10,650-foot Mt. Monashee, can be seen from roads, but getting there involves negotiating overgrown trails and fighting through jungles. However, logging roads are pushing deeper into the completely unprotected wildland and the air is full of noisy flutterbugs.

The Cariboos, which culminate in 11,550-foot Mt. Sir Wilfred Laurier, lie partly within Wells Gray and Bowron Lakes Provincial Parks, both reached by roads. The steep and thicket-tangled slopes and the raging, unbridged rivers and the lack of trails would keep the high country lonesome, except (1) new logging roads are constantly eroding the wilderness and (2) nobody *walks* into these ranges anymore, everyone *helicopters*.

Hiking

Helicopters give access to flower-bright meadows and alpine lakes and stunning views of sprawling glaciers. A person who objects to the existence of choppers is better off not walking at all but sitting down and letting his arms do the work, paddling a canoe. Resembling Paul Bunyan's Round River, in Bowron Lakes Park a group of lakes provides a circle trip of seven to ten days. Legs and back get their share of exercise in the seven portages, one 2 miles long. The circuit is terribly crowded in July and August and thus is best done earlier or later. Canoeists can gain more solitude in Wells Gray Park, putting in from the road-end at the outlet of Clearwater Lake, pushing and pulling from its inlet up the Clearwater River, then enjoying the quiet of Azure Lake.

Climbing

Wilderness mountaineering was superb throughout the Monashees and Cariboos before the air age but now is essentially nonexistent. Many peaks are simple snow walks or rock scrambles, numerous others offer good sport.

The Premier Range in the Cariboos is the most popular area and some climbers even walk in. Access is fairly easy from Tête Jaune Cache railway station on Highway 5 via a logging road, then faint trail, and finally gravel bars up Tête Creek to the Tête Glacier, above which towers Mt. Sir

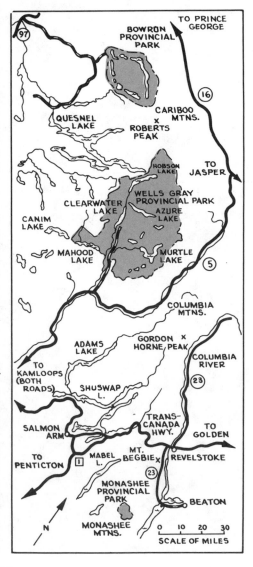

Wilfred Laurier, a long ascent on steep glacier and rock.

Hiking Season

The lush brush and broad glaciers convey a message—the climate is wet. Though not as drenched as coastal ranges, the Monashees and Cariboos alternate between sunshine and storm from July to October, the weather about a 50-50 mixture.

Mt. Begbie from Mt. Revelstoke, Monashee Mountains

GLACIER AND MT. REVELSTOKE NATIONAL PARKS

Administered by Mt. Revelstoke and Glacier
  National Parks and B.C. Forest Service
Fire permit required
Best season—July through September
Hiking—excellent
Climbing—excellent
Trail maps—park handouts are inadequate for
  hikers
*Guidebook—***Climber's Guide to the Interior Ranges of British Columbia**

Tall wedges of sky-splitting rock, icefields miles long and wide, acres of alpine flowers, loud rivers tumbling from raw moraines through lovely forest. A portion of the Selkirk Mountains lie in Mt. Revelstoke and Glacier National Parks; the rest is unprotected except by its own bulwarks, which increasingly are breached by loggers' bulldozers. Several parts are easy to enter and very popular, others are lonesome wilderness penetrated only by the most determined mountaineers.

The Selkirk Mountains are enclosed by the Big Bend of the Columbia River. Both parks are readily accessible from Highway 1, which crosses the range at 4341-foot Rogers Pass.

Hiking

Mt. Revelstoke Park

A road leads to the top of 6375-foot Mt. Revelstoke and splendid views west over the Columbia River to the Monashee Mountains and east into Glacier National Park. From the road-end a 5½-mile trail traverses a meadow ridge past Miller and Eva Lakes to Jade Lakes and close looks at glaciers and the park's highest peak, 8620-foot Mt. Coursier. The flower show is best in late July and early August. Overnight hikers must obtain fire permits from the park warden.

Glacier Park

A number of fine hikes begin from the Rogers Pass area. Trails typically are short and steep, built for sturdy 19th century folk in a hurry to reach the high country.

Abbott Crest. Dramatic views of Mt. Sir Donald, Rogers Pass, and countless glacier-covered peaks from a 7500-foot ridge. The trail starts near Illecillewaet Campground and climbs

3200 feet in 5 miles. At 2½ miles (just past Marion Lake) the path splits. The right fork ("shortcut trail") saves a mile by ascending directly to the crest. The left fork traverses hillside forest before opening into heather gardens. The 8091-foot summit of Abbott Peak is a delightful wander through rocks and flowers along the ridge.

Hermit Hut. Though the old log hut on the side of Mt. Sifton is not an important climbers' basecamp nowadays, views are as grand as ever and well worth an overnight stay. From the road at Rogers Pass the trail climbs a stiff 2400 feet in 1¾ miles.

Climbing

Before the Canadian Pacific Railway shifted its tourist emphasis to Banff and Lake Louise, Rogers Pass was the center of Canadian alpinism—luxurious Glacier House, imported Swiss guides, and all. The Selkirks still are preferred to the Rockies by connoisseurs of sound rock. Climbers must register with the park warden.

The Rogers Pass vicinity has enough peaks to keep a party busy and happy for weeks, the climbing generally on exceptionally beautiful and superbly solid quartzite. The highest is 10,818-foot Mt. Sir Donald, which offers a number of routes, none easy and some very difficult; the classic ascent is the Northwest Ridge, 3000 feet of Class 3 scrambling up an airy staircase.

The Dawson and Purity Ranges and others to the south require long mountaineering traverses

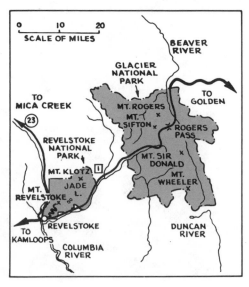

over icefields, down into and up out of deep cirques, and are so uncommonly visited as to seem more legend than reality—at least this was the case before the era of the cheap helicopter ride.

North of the park is a large area of equal splendor and greater remoteness, strictly for the wilderness mountaineer skilled in navigating vague routes. The highest summit of the Selkirks, 11,580-foot Mt. Sir Sanford, is guarded on its easiest side by a long and tricky slope of steep ice. The sheer granite walls of peaks around the Adamant cirque, centered on 11,040-foot Mt. Adamant, are among the continent's most impressive, comparable to the Bugaboos.

Hiking Season

Trails are usually open in early July, though snowpatches remain through the middle of the month; winter whiteness doesn't finally close up the shop until October. Weather is wetter than in the Rockies but in July and August the odds are that any given week will have a day or three of blue skies between rains and drizzles. Occasionally a whole week is sunny.

Mt. Sir Donald

PURCELL RANGE

Administered by B.C. Forest Service
Best season – July through September
Hiking – excellent but mostly rough
Climbing – excellent
Trail map – unknown
Guidebooks – Climber's Guide to the Interior
  Ranges of British Columbia, Exploring
  Purcell Wilderness

The Purcell Range is still another magnificent wilderness range, the rough and icy back country rarely visited except by helicopter. However, a few trails exist and the plundering of forests in this totally unprotected wonderland has resulted in a number of roads up entry valleys.

The Purcell Range lies west of the Columbia River on its northward flow to the Big Bend and is reached from Highway 95.

Hiking

Since roads change yearly, what with more logging and more washouts, hikers should seek current information at the Invermere and Spillimacheen stations of the B.C. Forest Service. Most trails are unmarked.

With the exception of the Bugaboo area, where a commercial operation and hordes of climbers maintain something of a trail system, the hiking is *not* of the "cookbook" type. Logging roads and bridges are built, abandoned, and washed out. If a trail is built it quickly brushes in. When a spot gains a degree of popularity, the grizzly bears turn surly. All in all, even a simple hike is something of an expedition, strictly for experienced wilderness travelers.

Bugaboos

From Brisco drive Bugaboo Creek road to 5000-foot Bugaboo Lodge, which serves well-heeled hikers and climbers. Poor folk can find campsites along Bugaboo Pass road. A number of trails built or improved by the lodge management lead to a variety of glories.

Bugaboo Pass. Noted for flowers. The prospectors' road to the 7400-foot pass can be driven only partway so hiking distance varies from ½-3 miles. Sun-exposed ridges blossom in June but mid-August usually puts on the best show.

Blue Lake. A 6-mile trail from the lodge climbs 2500 feet to a lake rimmed by a glacier.

Rocky Point. An old trail rebuilt by lodge employees for horse trips climbs 3000 feet in 10 miles to a 7500-foot viewpoint of the huge Vowell Glacier. The ridgecrest can be followed 8 miles from the trail-end to Blue Lake, climbing over several 8000-foot bumps, the entire way through meadows with a constant succession of gasping-and-gulping-type views.

Frenchman Mountain. A steep trail climbs 2900 feet in about 4 miles to a staggering look at the Bugaboos. The path quits at timberline; from there pick a route to the 7900-foot summit. The peak on the left offers the best views of the Quintet Peaks, the one on the right of Bugaboo Glacier. The ridge of shattered boulders between the peaks can be scrambled by experienced hikers.

Climbing

The Purcell back country offers wilderness mountaineers solitude as pure (or helicopter-impure) as that of neighboring ranges and a choice of walk-ups and stiff workouts on ice and rock. The highest peak of the Purcells is 11,343-foot Mt. Farnham.

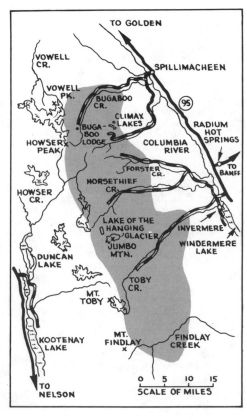

Thousands of climbers dream (some have nightmares) about the unbelievably sheer granite spires leaping from glaciers—the Bugaboos. Bugaboo Spire, Snowpatch Spire, and North Tower of Howser Spire—at 11,150 feet the highest of the group—are names to conjure with. Several summits can be reached by alpinists of modest skills, others are tough by the simplest way, and a number of walls invariably are included in any list of North American classics.

Hiking Season

The high country is usually snowbound until early or middle July. Rivers are flooded by snowmelt until late August, an important consideration if one must be forded to reach an objective. As in companion ranges, summer weather is messy. July, August, and September are partly sunny but rain may continue several weeks without a break; September almost invariably opens with a prolonged, vicious storm.

Commander Mountain and Lake of the Hanging Glacier

Canadian Rockies

(Above) Waterfowl Lake, Banff National Park
(Opposite) Mt. Robson and the Tumbling Glacier, Mt. Robson Provincial Park

Mountain goats, Jasper National Park

CANADIAN ROCKIES

1. Waterton Lakes National Park
2. Mt. Assiniboine Provincial Park
3. Banff National Park
4. Kootenay and Yoho National Parks
5. Columbia Icefield
6. Jasper National Park
7. Mt. Robson Provincial Park

Not to belittle the south-of-the-border prelude, in Canada the Rocky Mountains achieve their surpassing climax. So enormous is the sheer quantity of scenic wealth that most of the range has been blithely delivered to loggers and strip-miners and dammers. Luckily, though, decades before exploiters arrived in force one of North America's grandest systems of parks already had been dedicated. Conservationists working to achieve proper protection for the rest of the Canadian Rockies are consoled and inspired by the continuous parkland 250 miles long and 20-60 miles wide.

The beauties are easily seen. The Banff-Jasper Highway is one breathtaking experience after another and tourists not totally jaded by roadside views can ride snowmobiles up the Columbia Icefield, gondolas to fabulous panoramas, and helicopters everywhere.

Why bother to hike, then? Because from a machine one may *see* but never deeply *feel*. Despite roads, despite fame, the Canadian Rockies are so vast the walker can find whatever degree of private quiet he seeks. For those who want a little,

plus comforts unusual for wildland pedestrians in the Western Hemisphere, there are back-country lodges. For those who want as much as they can get there are long trails into wilderness defended against casual entry to wide and violent and unbridged rivers.

The climbers who flock by the thousands from around the world crowd only a few mountains, leaving hundreds of others alone. Most of the great routes are mainly or entirely on ice, some very steep; the sedimentary structures by and large are too loose to delight rock connoisseurs. Banff is headquarters for a number of guides, some independent, others under Banff Alpine Guides, P.O. Box 1025, Banff, Alberta.

The camping permits required in the parks, and the climbing permits for off-trail travel, may be obtained at Banff Fire Hall, Lake Louise Information Office, Columbia Icefield Visitor Center, Jasper Fire Hall, and warden stations.

Hiking ordinarily gets underway in the second half of June and continues through October. June is often cold and clear but can be steadily miserable. July and August are generally fair and hot with frequent afternoon thunderstorms; an occasional summer is rainy from start to end. Some Augusts the sky is obscured by smoke and about one year in three all trails are closed by fire danger; other times travel is permitted but campfires banned. September and early October frequently offer the best hiking, the days bright and the nights freezing.

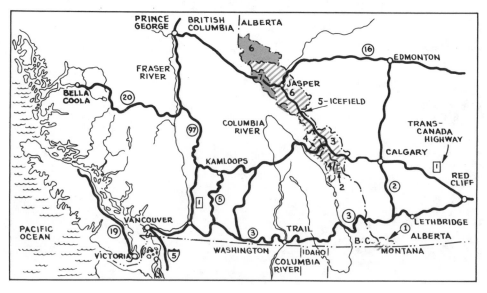

Upper Waterton Lake, Waterton Lakes National Park

WATERTON LAKES
NATIONAL PARK

Administered by Waterton Lakes National Park
Camping permit required
Best season—July through September
Hiking—excellent
Climbing—poor
Trail map—special handout for hikers
Guidebooks—Canadian Rockies Trail Guide,
    Rhule's Guide

Waterton Lakes National Park is similar to adjacent U.S. Glacier National Park, containing forest-rimmed lakes, abrupt cliffs, and alpine flower fields, including acres of beargrass climaxing bloom in late July. A unique feature of the park is that within its confines the Rocky Mountains and Great Plains meet—and indeed, here is one of the continent's few preserved samples of undisturbed short-grass prairie.

Highways lead to the park from Calgary and Lethbridge in Alberta and Great Falls in Montana.

Hiking

Though relatively small, the park has over 110 miles of some of the best trails in the Northwest, offering a variety of good overnight and day hikes. All back-country campers and climbers are required to obtain a permit at the information center or from the park wardens. Permits cannot be obtained here for camping in Glacier National Park.

Along with interesting short trails like Bear's Hump, Red Rock Canyon, and Blakiston Falls, two popular day-long hikes are to Crypt Lake (often very crowded) and Carthew Pass.

The hike to *Crypt Lake* is a most unusual combination—a boat ride, waterfalls, an alpine lake, and a 60-foot tunnel. From Waterton townsite take a Shoreline Cruise tour boat to Crypt Landing and arrange with the operator for a later pickup there. The 5½-mile trail climbs 2300 feet to the lake, the way easy enough but the tunnel and a short section of trail on the lake side are not recommended for claustrophobics or acrophobics.

Alderson-Carthew Trail. Glorious views of Waterton Lakes and far down the mountain chain into the United States are attained by ascending 2300 feet in 5 miles to the 7700-foot Carthew Pass. From Waterton townsite drive to Cameron Lake. The trail, starting on the east side of the outlet stream, reaches Summit Lake in 2½ miles, then climbs in earnest adjacent to the tops of the mountains. If transportation can be arranged, a hiker can continue on the trail, passing several high lakes and descending Carthew Creek to Waterton townsite, a total one-way distance of 12½ miles.

Climbing

Most peaks, including the highest, 9600-foot Mt. Blakiston, have walk-up sides. The faces are too rotten to attract climbers.

Hiking Season

Meadow trails usually are passable, though with lingering snowpatches, by mid-June and remain open through October. June is generally rainy, July and August dry with a very few thunderstorms and occasional strong winds. September and October are maybe good, maybe bad, maybe terrible, often good hiking months with clear days and cool nights. Strong winds are a common feature of late fall and spring months in Waterton.

The park is open year around. Chinook winds often open hiking trails even in midwinter.

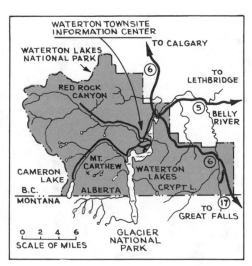

Mt. Custer and Summit Lake

MT. ASSINIBOINE PROVINCIAL PARK

Administered by Mt. Assiniboine Provincial Park
Best season – July through September
Hiking – excellent
Climbing – excellent
Trail map – Banff National Park (inadequate for hikers)
Guidebooks – 95 Hikes in the Canadian Rockies, Canadian Rockies Trail Guide, Climber's Guide to the Rocky Mountains of Canada

A tiny park by comparison with the neighbors but within it a hiker gazes upon miles of forests and alpine meadows, six glaciers and 11 lakes—if he can take his eyes off 11,870-foot Mt. Assiniboine, "the Matterhorn of Canada."

The park, located south of the town of Banff, is untouched by roads, accessible solely by trail. (The British Columbia government is considering building a road which would remove Assiniboine from wildness and add it to the endless array of spectacles already available for viewing along Canadian Rockies highways.)

Hiking

The loveliest spot is 7150-foot Lake Magog, at timberline below the glaciers and cliffs of Assiniboine. Two routes, both long, lead to the delightful, remote basin.

Spray Reservoir approach. Regular passenger cars must stop at a spillway 4 miles from the trailhead. Some hardy vehicles can continue to the road-end at the reservoir. Two trails to Lake Magog begin at the reservoir, one ascending easily over Assiniboine Pass, the other more spectacularly over Wonder Pass, offering views of Lake Gloria and Mt. Aye but for 5 waterless miles exposed to glaring sun. Each trail is 13 miles long and gains about 2500 feet. The best plan is to hike in over Assiniboine Pass, return over Wonder Pass.

Sunshine Village approach. The choice of most folks because of the decent access road. The trail is longer—18 miles—but gentler, gaining 1200 and losing 1600 feet. A two-day entry is customary.

All trails end at Mt. Assiniboine Lodge near the lakeshore. The lodge is horsey but does accept hikers; for reservations (essential) write Mt. Assiniboine Lodge, P.O. Box 369, Banff,

Alberta. The camp area is another mile around the west side of the lake. Views are magnificent.

Climbing

The ascent of Assiniboine is a classic, the walls tall and steep and the rock sufficiently sound to be sporting rather than suicidal. Difficulty depends on the weather. Some years a dozen parties reach the top; other ·summers the rock is continuously ice-plastered and defeats every attempt.

Hiking Season

Trails to Lake Magog generally are snowfree enough for hiking from early July through September.

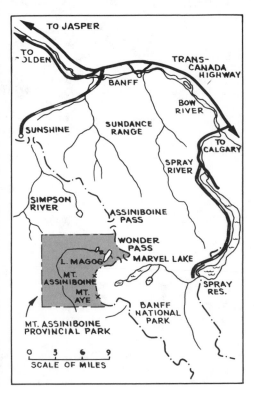

Mt. Assiniboine and Earling Strom's lodge at Magog Lake

BANFF NATIONAL PARK

Administered by Banff National Park
Camping permit required
Best season–July through September
Hiking–excellent
Climbing–excellent
Trail map–park handout is inadequate for hikers
Guidebooks–95 Hikes in the Canadian Rockies,
  Canadian Rockies Trail Guide, Climber's
  Guide to the Rocky Mountains of Canada

Banff was Canada's first national park, established in 1887, and is among the most famous and favorite mountain areas in North America. A hiker, aghast at the plush accommodations and tourist hordes of Banff City and Lake Louise, may not believe it possible to escape mobs anywhere in the vicinity. However, a few walking miles give a degree of peace and the back country is vast and empty.

Banff National Park is crossed by the Trans-Canada Highway and traversed by the Banff-Jasper Highway.

Hiking

The 700-plus miles of trails lead to alpine valleys, lakes, and the edges of some of the park's abundant glaciers. The problem is deciding where to go first.

Two easy day walks begin at 6190-foot Moraine Lake, in the Valley of the Ten Peaks; to Consolation Lake; to Larch Valley, colorful in fall, though by late September in perpetual shadow of surrounding peaks. A longer trip, starting from the road to Moraine Lake, is to flower-filled meadows of Paradise Valley. Egypt Lake, with numerous neighboring alpine lakes and pretty views, is a long day or overnight hike from the Bourgeau or Sunshine parking lot on the Banff-Jasper Highway. Do not expect to be lonesome on these deservedly popular trails.

To get away from it all try Freshfield Icefield, a great white sprawl amid giant peaks, protected from the madding crowd by a trail distance of 20-odd rough miles. One of the several approaches starts a bit north of the intersection of Banff-Jasper Highway and Highway 11 and goes up Howse River on a good path with several fords. Before setting out ask the park warden about current trail conditions.

Climbing

The climber's imagination is stimulated by scores of peaks offering routes ranging from hands-in-pockets to experts-only. The rock is mainly very rotten, discouraging frontal assaults on big faces and nearly everywhere more to be endured than enjoyed. Ice climbing on glaciers and early-summer snow covering rubble is the preferred sport.

Mt. Victoria, 11,365 feet, usually is climbed after an overnight stay in the stone hut at 9500-foot Abbott Pass, reached either from Lake Louise via trail and glacier or from Lake O'Hara via trail, snow, and scree. The route from the pass is up crumbling ledges and steep snowfields to the south ridge, then along a knife-edge of snow to the final series of crumbling ledges.

Stupendous Mt. Temple, 11,626 feet, has a scrambling side.

Hiking Season

Many trails are snowfree by mid-June and not blocked again until mid-October.

Mt. Chephren and Mistaya River

KOOTENAY AND YOHO NATIONAL PARKS

Administered by Kootenay and Yoho National Parks
Camping permit required
Best season – July through October
Hiking – excellent
Climbing – excellent
Trail map – park handouts are inadequate for hikers
Guidebooks – 95 Hikes in the Canadian Rockies, 84 Hikes in the Canadian Rockies, Canadian Rockies Trail Guides, Climber's Guide to the Rocky Mountains of Canada

The average tourist, driving pell-mell toward Banff or Lake Louise, is scarcely aware these two parks exist, though he does perhaps pause to snap a few photos of exciting peaks rising above green forests and clear rivers. Except at Lake O'Hara and Yoho Valley the trail population is relatively small.

Kootenay Park is traversed by the Banff-Windermere Highway, which crosses the Continental Divide from the Columbia River to the Bow River via Sinclair Pass and Vermilion Pass. Yoho Park is crossed by the Trans-Canada Highway over Kicking Horse Pass.

Advance reservations must be made for camps in the Lake O'Hara, Yoho Valley, and Tumbling Glacier areas.

Hiking

Kootenay Park

The 170 miles of trails are about as scenic as any and less crowded than most.

Stanley Glacier trail. The misnamed trail does not go near that particular glacier but in 3½ miles, gaining 900 feet, enters a nice little valley decorated by numerous hanging icechunks. Much of the way is through a 1968 burn which covered 4000 acres. Best views are from a rockslide above the trail-end. Find the trailhead on the Banff-Windermere Highway 3 miles west of Vermilion Pass.

Tumbling Glacier. An 8-mile hike gaining 2700 feet in forest and meadow to the glacier edge. Trail starts from Paint Pots parking area 6 miles west of Vermilion Pass.

Yoho Park

Though much of the 250-mile trail system is practically empty, the park contains two of the major hiker-and-climber magnets in the Canadian Rockies.

Lake O'Hara, 6700 feet, is reached from the Trans-Canada Highway near Kicking Horse Pass via an 8-mile "fire road," closed to private cars but traveled by a bus serving the small hotel at the lake. Hikers might as well pay the bus fare (high) and save energy for exploration. The campground lies ½ mile before the road-end. Trails radiate in every direction, some easy and crowded, some not.

A 2-mile path circles Lake O'Hara. A 3-mile trail, gaining 700 and losing 400 feet, leads to 7369-foot Lake McArthur, into which a glacier falls from Mt. Biddle. Emerald-green Lake Oesa, at 7800 feet beneath tremendous walls of Mt. Huber and Mt. Lefroy, is a 2½-mile walk gaining about 1000 feet. The Opabin Pass trail ascends in 2 miles to a group of beautiful tarns at 7400 feet under Mt. Biddle. Experienced hikers can follow a wildly-scenic high route connecting the tarns and Lake Oesa; the route is well-marked but quite rough and traverses some airy ledges.

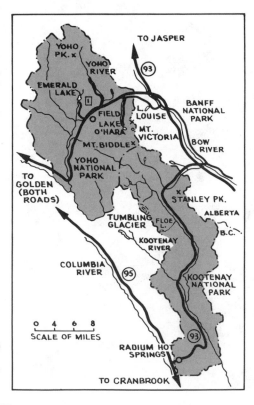

Yoho Valley is reached from the Trans-Canada Highway 4 miles east of Field via the Takakkaw Falls road. The best among several fine hikes is the Yoho Highline, a 15-mile loop trip from near the road-end. The up-and-down way, the highest elevation 6800 feet, passes through forest and flower gardens, by alpine lakes and raw moraines and white-water torrents, always with views of big peaks and glaciers.

Climbing

Though there are as good or better ascents in the back country, easy access and generations of publicity have made Lake O'Hara a busy, busy climbing center. Routes are mainly on rock—and the rock is mainly miserable. A number of peaks are walk-ups or scrambles. Victoria, Lefroy,

Huber, and others are sporting. The highest peak in the lake vicinity, 11,457-foot Mt. Hungabee, is a bear.

Yoho Valley climbing is largely on snow and glaciers. The President Range features gentle pleasures close to trails, 10,297-foot The President and 10,059-foot The Vice President being favorites. Slightly higher summits such as Balfour, Des Poilus, Gordon, and Collie are remote and lonesome and considerably more challenging.

Hiking Season

Forest trails generally are snowfree in early June and most higher paths by the end of the month. In mid-October winter begins to close the country.

Stanley Peak from Stanley Glacier trail, Kootenay National Park

COLUMBIA ICEFIELD

Administered by Banff and Jasper National
Parks
Camping permit required
Best season—June through September
Hiking—limited
Climbing—excellent
Trail maps—park handouts are inadequate for
hikers
Guidebooks— **94 Hikes in the Canadian Rockies,**
95 Hikes in the Canadian Rockies, Canadian
Rockies Trail Guide, Climber's Guide to the
Rocky Mountains of Canada

Completion of the 142-mile Banff-Jasper Highway in 1940 destroyed one of the continent's supreme wilderness walks and opened one of the world's sublimest mountain drives. The climax is on the boundary between Banff and Jasper National Parks at 6675-foot Sunwapta Pass, land of alpine meadows, stark peaks, and huge glaciers.

Covering 150 square miles, the Columbia Icefield is the largest in the Rockies; it is also the most accessible in North America. A road reaches the edge of the Athabasca Tongue of the Columbia Icefield and snowmobiles carry tourists miles over the surface. From the icefield's summit, 11,340-foot Snow Dome, glacier tongues flow into valleys on every side, their waters draining to the Pacific Ocean, Arctic Ocean, and Hudson Bay.

Hiking

Trails are few and short; this is climbers' country.

Parker Ridge. From the Banff side of Sunwapta Pass an easy path climbs less than 1000 feet to a view of the Saskatchewan Glacier.

Wilcox Pass. The trail starts near the campground and ascends meadows to a panorama of the icefield.

Climbing

Among the favorite climbs in the whole range, providing a broad overview of the icefield and remote valleys and peaks, is 11,452-foot Mt. Athabasca. The route, almost entirely up glaciers both steep and gentle, is easiest in June and July; in August hard ice melts out and greatly increases difficulty.

To ascend 12,294-foot Mt. Columbia and other noble peaks, backpack 8 miles up the Athabasca

Tongue to an icefield basecamp. In early summer skis or snowshoes are helpful.

Hiking Season

Trails are walkable July through September.

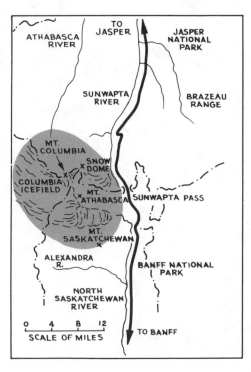

Summit ridge of Mt. Athabaska

JASPER NATIONAL PARK

Administered by Jasper National Park
Camping permit required
Best season – June to early October
Hiking – excellent
Climbing – excellent
Trail map – park handout is inadequate for hikers
Guidebooks – 94 Hikes in the Canadian Rockies,
   Canadian Rockies Trail Guide, Climber's
   Guide to the Rocky Mountains of Canada

By the time a highway traveler arrives from the south in Jasper National Park he is exhausted by seeing so much so fast, has nary a gasp or exclamation or superlative left. The cure for that is to take to the trails, the views coming singly and slowly expanding and shifting as the route passes forests and finger lakes in ice-gouged valleys, alpine meadows and tarns, animals large and small, and marvelous peaks and glaciers.

An indentation in the southwest side of Jasper Park is filled by Hamber Provincial Park; to the north, set aside for lonesomeness-lovers, is large and little-traveled Willmore Wilderness Provincial Park.

Hiking

The 600 miles of trails provide any sort of trip from short and easy family walks to long expeditions involving difficult river fords. Crowds there are in spots, but plenty of empty places too.

Tonquin Valley. One of the four most famous hikes in the Canadian Rockies, 12 miles to 6450-foot Amethyst Lake at the foot of The Ramparts. Starting at a trailhead 12.7 km up the Cavell Road, the trail gradually descends 500 feet to the Astoria River, steeply ascends 1700 feet over a shoulder of Oldhorn Mountain, and drops 700 feet to Amethyst Lake. Campgrounds are located at a number of spots along the way; advance reservations are necessary. A side-trip into the violence of Outpost Valley is worth the strenuous climb on rough trail.

Mt. Edith Cavell view. The trail begins as a paved path from the Edith Cavell parking lot. In ½ mile the way divides. Take the uphill fork, ascending moraine and forest to green meadows spattered with flowers. Trail ends at 2 miles. For closer looks at rock ramparts of the mountain wander higher to the ridge crest.

Climbing

Walk-ups, gentle and steep glaciers, and extremely difficult rock—Jasper Park has scores of routes for every ambition and ability. As elsewhere in the range, much of the rock is awful.

The favorite goal is 11,033-foot Mt. Edith Cavell, one of the most enjoyable snow, ice, and rock climbs in the Rockies and on just about eveybody's list of classics.

The numerous ice-and-rock peaks of Outpost Valley make it a popular climbing center. Impressive 11,386-foot Mt. Brazeau is reached from Maligne Lake, but not easily. Innumerable back-country summits intrigue the wilderness mountaineer.

Hiking Season

Valley trails generally are open in early June, higher paths by the end of the month. Winter returns in October.

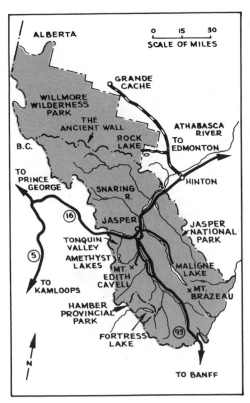

Mountain goats beside the Athabaska River

MT. ROBSON PROVINCIAL PARK

Administered by Mt. Robson Provincial Park
Best season–July through September
Hiking–good
Climbing–excellent
Trail map–park brochure
Guidebooks– **94 Hikes in the Canadian Rockies,**
 Canadian Rockies Trail Guide, Climber's
 Guide to the Rocky Mountains of Canada

Mt. Robson, at 12,972 feet the highest peak in the Canadian Rockies, stands summit and shoulders above neighbors. The highway gives impressive views of the bare south wall but the stupendous cliffs and glaciers can only be seen properly from the trail.

Hiking

Berg Lake is perhaps *the* classic hike in the range. The trail begins under the tremendous south face of Robson and in 12 miles swings around the mountain to the ice-speckled lake beneath the incredible north face. Scenery is splendid even if merely part of the route is walked—2 miles to quiet Kinney Lake surrounded by forest, 6 miles to White Falls in the Valley of a Thousand Falls, or a bit farther to spectacular Emperor Falls. However, Berg Lake is "the place." From the 5500-foot shore in timberline meadows a hiker looks over wind-rippled waters to icebergs breaking from the foot of Tumbling Glacier, then up and up an astoundingly-vertical 7500 feet to the summit.

Find the trailhead at the Mt. Robson viewpoint 53 miles west of Jasper townsite on Highway 16. The 12 miles gain a net of 2700 feet but much more in the gross. The miles are long partly because of the ups and downs and rough terrain. Six campgrounds are located along the trail.

A simple scramble up the ridge west of Berg Lake gives a more stunning panorama, if that is conceivable.

Climbing

By the easiest route Mt. Robson is one of the toughest peaks in the Canadian Rockies, cliffs and glaciers appallingly steep, snow conditions often impossible, storms sudden and severe. Some years the mountain is climbed a dozen times; others it repels every attempt.

Other fine ascents from Berg Lake, requiring less skill and nerve, include 11,171-foot Mt.

Resplendent and 11,101-foot Mt. Whitehorn. In addition there are good scrambles and pleasant walk-ups.

Hiking Season

Trips to Berg Lake are best planned for mid-July through September, though the first part of the trail is open in early June, not snow-closed until late October.

Mt. Robson and Berg Lake

INDEX

\